# Daily Affirmations

### For Adult Children of Alcoholics

Published by Health Communications, Inc.
Enterprise Center
3201 SW 15th Street
Deerfield Beach, FL 33442

ISBN 0-932194-27-3 ·

Printed in the United States of America.

First Printing, Soft Cover

# ACKNOWLEDGMENTS

With special appreciation for the contributions
of:

Barbara Naiditch
Lois Weisberg
Diane Halperin
Judith Bohnen
Linda Christensen
Evelyn Baron


Rokelle Lerner acknowledges the contributions
of those who helped to inspire this work:

Karen Kaiser-Clark
Ernie Larsen
Rusty Berkus
Alla Bosworth Campbell
Pamela Levin
Sondra Smalley
Jean Illsley-Clark
Herbert Gravitz
Julie Bowden
Jael Greenleaf
Sharon Wegscheider-Cruse
Claudia Black
Janet Woititz

Credits:

Mark Worden, Editor
Reta Kaufman, Illustrator

# INTRODUCTION

Affirmations are positive, powerful statements concerning the ways in which we desire to think, feel and behave. The meditations in this book cover many aspects of our existence and help us to paint a mental portrait of what we want to become. This book was written for adults who want to replace their critical inner dialogue with positive affirmations, and thereby improve their mental picture.

The messages which we give to ourselves are the most important messages we hear. The internal briefings and conversations we hold determine our attitudes, our behavior, and the course of our lives. If, as children, we were criticized and shamed, our internal dialogue will be self-depricating. If we are used to large doses of self-imposed sarcasm and negative reviews of our daily performance, we gradually mutilate our self-esteem, our creativity and our spirit.

As adult children of alcoholics, we can continue to remain in the past and believe the negatives which we were taught; or we can change our beliefs with affirmative thoughts which can set us free into better and more expansive experiences. What we choose to believe will ultimately rule our world. If we continue to believe we are victims—so we are. However, if we choose health, joy and love—we will have it. The choice is always ours. The shame and critical beliefs of the past gradually lose their power to limit us as we begin to see the futility in continuing them. Affirmations are a way to wake us up—to make us fully conscious and aware of the daily choices we make. And, as we learn to direct our thoughts, our feelings and behavior will naturally follow.

To use these messages effectively, read each affirmation aloud to yourself and repeat it several times. Then, slowly read the entire meditation aloud and reflect upon its meaning. For adult children of alcoholics' groups, choose one affirmation and read it to the entire group. Ask individuals not only to reflect upon its meaning, but to offer specific ways that they might incorporate the affirmation into their lives.

No longer is it necessary to dwell in the intensity of pain and despair. It is possible to feed the imagination with different thoughts and create a new way of living.

It is my hope that this book will mark a new beginning for those individuals who are ready to make the choice to accept joy and light into their lives.

*Rokelle Lerner*

## ABOUT THE AUTHOR

Rokelle Lerner is founder and co-director of Children Are People, Inc., a counseling, training and consulting firm in St. Paul, Minnesota. Children Are People has specialized in providing services to children and adults from alcoholic families for the past nine years. Rokelle also maintains a private practice for adults with addictive behaviors.

Rokelle is frequently featured as a primary speaker to discuss issues, thoughts and ideas of interest and relevance to children and adults who grew up in chemically dependent homes.

She is a founding board member and current treasurer of the National Association for Children of Alcoholics, and is an effective advocate for young COA's.

Rokelle was featured in the 1982 film **Hope for the Children.** In 1985, *Esquire* Magazine named her as one of America's outstanding young women who has made an extraordinary contribution to this country.

Rokelle lives with her husband and two daughters in St. Paul.

*NEW START*

# I WELCOME THIS NEW DAY AND THIS NEW YEAR

Today I have a fresh start. I choose to begin a new letting go of unhealthy thoughts, feelings and attitudes that have stifled my growth.

This day I choose to think new thoughts, to look at new values and to find new ways of expressing my God-given gifts.

I now choose to deepen my understanding of myself and others. I will look at my relationships with family and my friends in a new light. I choose to have vital, healthy interactions with others.

I truly welcome this new day, this new year, and this new me. I welcome the wonderful possibilities open to me.

*EXPECTATIONS*

## I HAVE WONDERFUL
## EXPECTATIONS OF THIS DAY

The day that stretches before me holds promise of much good. I have been given a blank piece of paper on which to write, and I will write only that which I lovingly wish for myself:

I expect today to be a day of renewal, a day of joy, a day of love and peace.

I expect this to be a day of healing; I expect to feel vibrant health surging through me.

I expect this day to be a day of joy, a day in which I feel free from anxiety. I expect this day to contain delightful surprises.

I expect this day to be a day of love. My personal relationships will be satisfying and fulfilling. I will not have to work hard to get my needs met.

I expect today to be filled with wonderful promise, and so it will be.

*FEELINGS*

### MY FEELINGS ARE
### TEMPORARY AND FLUID

Today I acknowledge that I have emotions—but I am more than my emotions. I recognize this day that I have thoughts, but I am more than my thoughts. I need not cling to uncomfortable feelings or negative thoughts today.

If I am feeling low in spirit for any reason, I must remember that the clouds will lift, the moods will pass, and I will see light again.

Nothing outside me has the power to keep me depressed or anxious. No person has the power to keep me upset or lonely. I have it in my power to choose what I believe about my feelings.

Today I choose to believe that my feelings are temporary and fluid.

Today I choose to believe that my spirits will rise above the clouds. My infinite source sustains me and I know my heart will again sing a joyous song.

---

*HEALTHY THOUGHTS*

## I FEEL FREE TO MOVE ON TO HEALTHIER IDEAS, THOUGHTS AND EMOTIONS

Today I rejoice in my ability to move on to new thoughts, new relationships, new emotions.

Many times in my family, I felt trapped, isolated and unable to see a way out. I did not know how to spring free from the emotions and behaviors of others.

But I know now that I cannot be responsible for my family. I love my family, but I must also live my own life, with self-respect and freedom.

I do not have to be trapped in unhealthy situations. I can make changes in myself, and I can strive to find ways to shrug off the traps that imprison me.

Today I will put all negativity behind me, and I will continue to be aware of my power to cope effectively with unhealthy situations.

*GOALS*

## *TODAY I WILL TAKE STEPS TOWARD ATTAINING MY GOALS*

Today I begin a journey toward reaching the goals I dream about so vividly. I will concentrate on clearly defining what I want in my relationships.

I will reflect on what I need in the physical, emotional and spiritual areas of my life, and I will take time today to take action on at least one of my goals.

I will not block myself from taking action. Too often in the past I have had hopes and dreams that were blocked by my lack of direction and by fear.

Today I have a sense of direction and the strength to make decisions in the face of fear. I will not allow myself to be paralyzed by indecision.

Instead, I will move with confidence, knowing that change is a series of small successes.

*BELIEFS*

### TODAY I OPEN MYSELF
### TO NEW BELIEFS

I feel no fear of new beliefs today. I see that changing my beliefs helps me release old patterns of behavior.

In my alcoholic home, I learned to view life in ways that were unhealthy for me. I acquired attitudes and beliefs about people that were unbalanced, distorted, and out of focus. These old beliefs are like blueprints from the past, but I realize that I can change them.

Today I give my strength and my power to new beliefs.

Today I know my life can change if I have faith and confidence, and if I truly believe it can change.

When my beliefs are tentative and half-hearted, my life is tentative and half-hearted. So I must believe with all my heart that healthy recovery, healthy relationships and a harmonious life are possible for me.

Today I give my strength and power to new beliefs.

*TENDER MOMENTS*

### I WILL BE HERE AND NOW AND REJOICE IN ALL THAT SURROUNDS ME

Let me be gentle today. Let me cast aside my protective shell, let me loosen my muscles and feel myself become less rigid, less brittle.

I smile as I feel myself move harmoniously with nature. My spirit flows from moment to moment. I am tender to myself, gentle, and I am aware of the gentleness hidden in others.

I take time to notice textures. I touch and am touched by soft currents of air. I listen to small sounds. I take delight in subtle tastes and smells.

I am present, here and now, and put aside past pain and fear. I let in the beauty that surrounds me, from moment to moment.

*APATHY-BE-GONE*

### I FREE MYSELF FROM APATHY

Today I will shake off my apathy, and I will free myself from the heavy feelings of powerlessness, helplessness and futility.

I realize that I might become apathetic if I think that my life has no meaning, has no possibility for growth and change. I see that my life has meaning and that there is always room for change, always a way to break free from the past.

I will no longer be dissatisfied and bogged down by what my parents did many yesterdays ago. I will not be paralyzed by what happened to me in the past. It is time to forgive, time to let go and move on.

I am not a victim. I am alive, wide awake and free from the numbness of apathy. I look forward to each new day with exhilaration, as I zestfully take on the challenges that come my way.

*ATTENTIVENESS*

## TODAY I WILL LISTEN ATTENTIVELY TO ALL THOSE I COME IN CONTACT WITH

I will listen to opinions, thoughts, and feelings, and will try to understand what people are saying with the words they use. I will not attempt to read minds or interpret what others say as judgments against me.

I will work hard today to accept others and not over-react when they voice an opinion or a feeling different from my own.

I grew up in a family where chaos and turbulent emotions were commonplace. I felt controlled by family members. But I no longer need to feel controlled by the emotions of others.

Today I will recognize my powerlessness over the thoughts, opinions, feelings and actions of others. I will work hard today to allow others to be who they are.

I will be who I am. I will listen attentively, noting others' perspectives calmly and appreciatively.

*POSITIVE ATTITUDE*

## I WILL AFFIRM MY WORTH AND GOODNESS AND OPEN MY EYES TO THE GOODNESS IN OTHERS

Today I will pay attention to the positive qualities of the people in my life. I will be more tolerant of human frailties and increase my awareness of the wonderful complexity of humankind.

In noticing the goodness of others, I affirm and claim my own. What kind of person am I? I am positive, loving, strong and capable. And others? I will look for their strong points, for their friendliness and for their resilience. I will understand that they were not put on earth to meet my needs unconditionally, just as I cannot unconditionally meet theirs.

I will strive to see the goodness in others, and appreciate their uniqueness.

*LOVE*

### *I WILL GIVE MY LOVE FREELY AND GENTLY*

Love will flow from me like rays of sunshine. Love is my total acceptance of me and you. Love is giving. Love is the glowing light within each person.

At times in the past, my love had been hidden, blocked off by inpenetrable clouds. No light or love came through. These clouds prevented me from seeing the love within me and the love within you.

Only I can dispel my clouds. Only I can let my radiance shine forth. Only I can show you my being.

In my family the love we felt for each other often got cloudy with broken promises, fear, anger and confusion. But today the confusion, anger and fear are gone. I no longer dwell on past broken promises.

Today I let my love shine forth, and I share my bounty with others.

*SELF-PACE*

### I WILL QUIET MY MIND AND BODY AND I WILL BE CALM IN THE KNOWLEDGE THAT I AM NOT ALONE

I will slow down today and take time for me. I will become emotionally calm. I will slow down physically, knowing that I can accomplish what has to be done without haste and frantic activity.

I slow down to pace myself, to appreciate the nuances of an unrushed life. Moving slowly, I am reminded of my special connection to my Higher Power. I feel touched with a kind of Godliness, and I am inspired.

Growing up in an alcoholic family, I kept busy with tasks, work, outside activities and school—immersed in action and crowds to avoid feeling lonely, isolated, and ashamed.

But now, I can slow down, I can take my time, and go at my own pace. I choose my company in a leisurely way, without a sense of obligation and urgency.

*SELF-RESPECT*

### TODAY I WILL BE AWARE OF MY OWN FEELINGS AND AFFIRM MY SELF-RESPECT

I see two kinds of fear: There is a healthy kind of fear that tells me when there are real dangers in the world to be wary of; this healthy fear protects me. But there is another kind of fear—the anxiety that I will not be able to live up to the expectations others might have of me.

Today I see that I do not have to strive continually to please others. I will please myself, I will take myself into consideration. I will take stock of my own needs and wants and know that I can choose to act fearlessly on my own.

I know my anxieties will lessen the more I respect my own needs and desires and make them known to others. I feel happy and peaceful in this knowledge.

*RULES*

## TODAY I WILL LOOK AT THE RULES I LIVE BY AND CHANGE THEM TO FIT THE PERSON I AM NOW

I see that I can choose to keep my current rules or change them. I can realign the guiding values in my life to make them relevant to who I am now.

I can recognize the importance of guidelines, rules, values—all the overt and covert principles which help guide my daily existence. I also recognize the need to evaluate the rules that have been passed down to me from parents and grandparents.

Today I will become more aware of the rules in my life. I will carefully assess them, knowing I can decide to keep them if they fit, or discard them if they are outdated or inappropriate.

My criterion shall be: Does this rule or guideline enhance my life and enable me to be a more creative and fulfilled person, or does it constrict my life and keep me bound to the past?

Rules are guidelines that confront me with my limits.

I can keep the rules from the past. Or I can rewrite them and choose guidelines that I can feel comfortable with. I have the power to make the choice.

**(14)**

*SELF-CARE*

### *TODAY I WILL RESPECT MY BODY, MY PHYSICAL SELF*

My body is a vital gift, and I will treat it with respect, with the utmost care. I will seek out what it means to truly nourish my body, and I will take special care to eat healthy meals.

Growing up in an alcoholic environment, I invested so much emotional energy in other people that I forgot to focus on the needs of my physical being. But today I will look at my habits and ask, "Do my habits promote health and well-being, or do they undermine it? Do I overeat, or undereat? Do I smoke, and through denial, contend that I'm invulnerable? Do I get enough rest and enough exercise?"

Today I will make a fearless and searching inventory of my physical being and do those things which show respect for my body, my physical self.

*THE CHILD IN ME*

### I WILL PAY ATTENTION
### TO THE CHILD IN ME

I am an adult, but I need to remind myself of the value of those child-like qualities I may have forgotten or pushed aside.

Like many others raised in alcoholic families, I gave up my childhood early. I became serious too soon. I became a caretaker, old for my years, responsible for adults in my family.

Today I will let my child surface and blend with my adult state. I feel a vibrant energy. Filled with wonder, I look at the world with fresh eyes. I can let myself laugh freely and spontaneously. I can be playful and experience the moment, perfectly centered, alert.

Today is a perfect day to notice how children play and how they interact with their environment. As my inner child surfaces, my rigidity melts away like icicles melting in the sun.

*SELF-TRUST*

## I WILL TRUST ALL MY OWN THOUGHTS AND EMOTIONS

Today I recognize strongly that I have no control over anyone's actions or emotions. I stand in this world with myself and with my Higher Power. I need to continue to relate to friends and family members and continue to grow in those relationships.

As I trust people with my intimate self, I need to trust my self, my own thoughts and my own emotions. Growing up in an alcoholic family, I often discounted my own thoughts and emotions. In trying so hard to please others, I made myself unhappy.

Today I need to affirm trust in myself and trust in my Higher Power, so that I will continue to validate my own thoughts and my own emotions.

I will validate and trust my own thoughts and emotions today.

*SUCCESS*

### *I MAKE DECISIONS CONFIDENTLY*

I will feel confident with each decision I make. I take special care to make decisions based on what I know now. I will make decisions confidently and at my own pace. I will not be ruled by impulsiveness or be pressured into making a decision before I'm ready.

At the same time, I will have no fear of making decisions because each decision will be made with deliberation and in good faith.

In the past, I let decisions pile up. I put them on "hold" because I was anxious about making a mistake. Today I know that I will make the best choices I can possibly make. I am allowed to make mistakes, and I am allowed to learn from them.

I cannot live without making decisions. Knowing this, I will make decisions confidently and without fear. I will trust my decisions and do the best I can.

*PARENTS*

### I ACCEPT MY PARENTS AND AFFIRM MY INDEPENDENCE FROM THEM

Today I will live my life as a person independent from my parents. My parents are separate people, with their own thoughts, emotions and behaviors. They do not control me and I do not control them.

I have my own thoughts, emotions and behavior. I am independent, but I care for my parents and I do not condemn them. They have their shortcomings and faults, as I have mine. My parents have praiseworthy qualities and they do the best they can, as I do the best I can. I will no longer try to change their thoughts and emotions.

My task today is to affirm my independence and to see the positive characteristics in my parents.

*OPPORTUNITIES*

## I CAN MEET NEW OPPORTUNITIES WITHOUT FEAR

I will be alert and open to new opportunities today. I will view them with a positive attitude and I will not allow myself to be stifled by my anxieties.

I see that anxiety comes from growing up in an insecure, alcoholic environment where I never had any control over the bad things that happened. But that was then, and this is now. I can unhook from the past, unhook from the turbulent feelings, and unhook from the anxieties that have plagued me.

If my apprehension and anxiety persist, I will seek ways to reduce my reactions to the past. I will take steps to learn relaxation and stress management. I will unlearn the beliefs that hold me back.

I will not be intimidated by the past or held in bondage to it. I will become my own person and greet the opportunities which each day brings.

*FRIENDSHIP*

### I WILL SEEK OUT FRIENDS TODAY, THE SPECIAL PEOPLE IN MY LIFE

Today I will surround myself with people who care about me. I take deep satisfaction in knowing there are people in my life I can turn to. I, too, can be a friend—I can give support and nurturing to others without becoming responsible for their lives. In the past, I avoided friendships because they became too painful, too demanding. I expected too much of myself and I expected too much of others. I now realize that I no longer need to isolate myself from friendships. I cannot solve the problems of my friends, and they cannot solve mine. But we can give each other support, we can listen, we can care for each other.

Today feels like a good time to call up a friend, or to make contact with an old friend whom I haven't seen for some time. Friendship and recovery go hand-in-hand.

*MY INNER SELF*

### I WILL CULTIVATE AND LISTEN TO MY INTUITIVE SELF

Today I will delve inward and explore my inner spaces. I will become more aware of my intuitive voice to guide me throughout the day. I will experience peace and joy today, and listen to the wise part of myself.

Many times I search for this peace and never find it. I am too busy trying to control outside forces, trying to control people, and trying to predict outcomes. I never seem to get enough of what I want.

I know my fulfillment wells from within, flows from my inner self, independent of outside events. I will listen to my intuitive self today, and center in on me.

*LETTING GO*

### *I WILL LET GO OF THE PAST AND WILL LET MY WOUNDS HEAL*

I will transcend the pain I've carried from the past. When hurt, I erected barriers, strong walls to protect me and help me feel secure.

Today is a new day, a day to go beyond the painful barriers that gave me an illusion of safety. I scrutinize the barriers. I examine them, and say, **Yes, they were important to me once. The were useful back then. But no more.**

I no longer need the heritage of hurt that keeps me from full enjoyment of the present. Barriers down, confident and alert to what the new day brings, I do not dwell on the past. I am no longer limited by fear and apprehension. I can move freely. Renewed and resolute, I look for new directions and new challenges. I feel joy and peace in the present moment.

*POWER WORDS*

### I WILL USE WORDS WHICH EMANATE POWER, STRONG WORDS TO GUIDE ME

My words today will be strong and powerful. I will choose words that convey a sense of mastery, competence, and ability: **I can. I will. I am. I do ...**

I will not limit myself by using words that convey indecision and weakness. I will avoid saying: "I can't." "It's impossible." "No way ..." "I'm not smart enough." "I give up."

Today I'm on the lookout for self-defeating messages sent from me ... to myself, welling forth from my inner self in a stream of negative chatter. Today I will end the negative chatter. I see that I can change negative thoughts into positive ones as I am able make changes within myself. I can choose words of power to help create a new perspective on life, and a new perspective on myself.

*FULFILLMENT*

### I FEEL COMPLETE TODAY, FULFILLED AND LOVED

This morning I feel great hope and great potential for myself. I feel energized by the love I feel around me. I will pay attention to all the good there is for me today. I will build on all the positive aspects of my life and pass them on to tomorrow.

Today I will not brood on self-limitations. I will be fully present and fully alive and alert to the potential of all people. And in sensing the potential of all, I will more completely grasp my own.

I feel surrounded by love as my hopes take firm root in reality. I can make things happen, I can actualize my potential. Through love and being loved, I can grow and become fulfilled.

*HAPPINESS FOUND*

## I CREATE MY OWN HAPPINESS

I am the creator of my own joy and happiness. Today I recognize that I will not find happiness by waiting for it to happen, or by having it bestowed upon me by a happiness benefactor. I find joy in who I am, and I relish what life has to offer.

True happiness does not come from externals. True happiness does not come from flashy cars, stylish clothes, and expensive homes. I do not need "the right person" to make me happy, nor do I search for happiness the way I search for a lost set of keys.

I define happiness for myself. I make my own happiness today and experience joy in living in my own unique way.

*BEING RESOURCEFUL*

## I AM A RESOURCEFUL PERSON

I take stock of my resourcefulness today. I can achieve goals, I can get things done. I can take care of business so that I can feel free to enjoy other important aspects of my life.

No more evasion today. No more procrastination.

Today I do what needs to be done. I take charge of unpleasant tasks I have put off. I make clear, definite plans to resolve them, and I like the feeling that comes with accomplishment. It frees me, and I can move on, I can take the time to enjoy my own creativeness without stewing over unfinished business.

GROWTH

## I SEE THE MANY THINGS
## I CAN LEARN FROM OTHERS

I will be aware today of all that I can learn from others. I appreciate the variety I see in others, the different skills, abilities, wisdom and special intelligence.

I observe the emotional responses of others and I see there is no single "right way" for everyone. I freely look at different viewpoints without feeling threatened, without feeling that I must relinquish my own thoughts and beliefs.

I feel lucky for being able to experience diversity, and I feel fortunate in sharing the many facets of other people's lives. I feel relaxed and nonjudgmental about the diversity around me as I learn from the wisdom and experience of others.

*SENSUAL LIFE*

## *I WILL OPEN MY SENSES TO THE BEAUTY THAT SURROUNDS ME*

Today is a day to revel in my sensual being. I participate in life today, with my senses open, alert, receptive.

So often as I was growing up in my alcoholic family, I found my vision clouded, my hearing stunned, and my sense of touch numbed.

Today I am a new person. I will take special care to open my eyes to the beauty of nature. I will notice the free-form artistry of clouds and the wizardry of trees and leaves. I see colors, shapes and shades.

I listen to sounds, to the murmur of voices, the mood of music, the rustle of fabric and the hushed flow of air. I taste flavors and I savor my food.

I touch those near to me with love and gentleness, and I am touched in return. I cherish the texture of touch, the texture of life.

CONTROL

## I AM LEARNING TO FLOW WITH THE CURRENT OF LIFE

I relinquish my struggle to control today. I give up efforts to dominate life. I no longer feel the need to force things to happen my way. I no longer need to hold on, to control.

Just as the river has powerful currents, life, too, has strong forces that pull and tug. And just as the leaf in the river survives by going with the flow, I, too, will go with the flow of life.

The river flows around boulders, obstacles and obstructions, and I, too, will find my course around obstructions and frustrations in my life. I have survived the forces that would have weakened or even annihilated me, and I have sprung free and open to the beauty of life.

*AWARENESS*

### I AM RENEWED AND REFRESHED IN MY NEW AWARENESS

I have a new awareness in my life, a lightning-borne, electrical awareness that I am free to deal with the past. I am free to come to terms with the painful fact that I grew up in an alcoholic home. As the adult child of an alcoholic, I realize that I was affected by my family in many ways. Even as an adult, I feel anxious and afraid, just as a child fears lightning.

But sometimes lightning brings a bright flash that illuminates the darkness, and we can see where we are. A lightning storm may make us feel isolated, anxious and afraid, but after the storm, we feel renewed and refreshed.

I now know that I can choose to deal with this new awareness or let it rest. After this blinding truth revealed itself, I realized I could never be the same person.

I am enlightened, exhilarated, and I am freer than ever to put the past behind me and do what needs to be done.

*NEEDS*

## I ACKNOWLEDGE MY NEEDS TODAY, AND I FEEL FREE TO MAKE THEM KNOWN

I have needs, and it is all right to meet those needs without feeling guilty and ashamed. I will take the risk today to express myself and my needs to those I trust.

I will face the frightening voices from the past that tell me I am unworthy and threaten me. This day I answer those voices, I move far beyond them and gradually reveal my needs to those who care.

I understand fully that no one can fill my emptiness, no single person can make me feel complete. Even when I make my needs known, others will not always answer. Sometimes they cannot.

Today I realize that even those who care about me most cannot read my mind. My needs will not go unnoticed today as I begin to make them known.

*SERENITY*

### I ALLOW MY HIGHER POWER TO ENTER MY LIFE TODAY, AND CHERISH THE SERENITY THAT FOLLOWS

Today I will set aside my ego and I will realize that I have an undeniable connection with a Higher Power. The connection is renewed by insightful discoveries, in moments when I am stirred beyond words, and during instants of wonder and amazement.

I trust the serenity my Higher Power provides. I am in touch with the irrefutable reality that life has meaning—all life, My life. I rejoice in being a part of the universe. I am cared for and protected by my Higher Power.

*HOPE*

### I CAN MAKE MY DREAMS BECOME REALITY

I have dreams and wishes and I know that I can work towards making those dreams and wishes come true. Visualizing the future, I have an attitude of hopeful expectancy. I delight in challenges that bring out the best in me.

In my alcoholic family my hopes took the form of fantasies. I hoped for magical cures and miraculous changes. I wanted family members to behave differently. I dreaded the future and hoped that next week would somehow be better. Or next month. Or next year. I prayed that some external force would make life more bearable.

But now I've gradually learned that the only changes I can control are changes in myself. I can change, I can control my reactions to people and to events.

Today I will focus on what I can do to start making my hopes become realities.

PEACE

## I AM AT PEACE WITHIN MYSELF, CALM AND TRANQUIL

I am composed today, and I feel the inner harmony and the inner peace that come with balance. Alert and confident, I face stresses and pressures, knowing that I can quiet turbulent emotions, I can calm my racing thoughts.

Today I will take time to release the tension I feel—through physical activity, meditation, prayer, or another form of self-affirmation. I let myself relax and feel the tension flow out of my muscles. All anxiety vanishes as I center myself and experience the peace of my Higher Power.

I will carry this inner peace with me into every activity today. I remain calm and composed, in control of my thoughts and words, my actions and reactions.

No matter what transpires today, I know that nothing—no person, no situation—can disturb my calm and peace, my serenity.

*SURRENDER*

## *LOVE IS FOR ME*

I can surrender to love and still preserve my independence. Surrendering to love does not mean I have to surrender my convictions, values, or integrity. I only do this when I need love so desperately that I become in danger of giving myself away entirely. When I worry about losing myself in love, it usually means that my sense of personal identity is fragile.

When I am in love, I allow that person to enter that private world within me. I allow that person to matter at the deepest level of my being. I do not surrender myself to the other person; I surrender to **my feelings** for the other person. It is a disastrous error to think that I will lose or gain my identity in a relationship. I do not approach relationships with the belief that love can fill a vacuum of identity. Love is for people who know who they are. Love is for me.

*COURAGE*

### FEARLESSLY, I FACE MY FEARS

Today I will examine my fears without anxiety. Fear, more than anything else, can hold me in bondage. Fear can place chains around my soul and slow down my progress in life.

I can conquer fear. I can face my fears and work to overcome them.

I place my fears in the hands of my Higher Power, and fear diminishes, fear loses its hold on me. Centered in my Higher Power, I am free from worry and anxiety.

Today I release the small nagging fears and the overpowering threats that seem to have me in a vise.

Today I remember that I shall not fear, for God is with me.

*COURAGE*

## *I POSSESS THE COURAGE TO CHOOSE THE DIRECTION OF MY LIFE*

I can live the kind of life that the deepest part of me desires. I have the courage to choose the direction of my life. I have the courage to make decisions which will enhance my life, and I have the willingness to act upon my decisions.

I am on a voyage of discovery. I am discovering the core issues that prevent me from enjoying life. I am discovering the specific fears that inhibit the growth of my full potential.

I am discovering my motivations and intentions so that I can make clear decisions about my life. All of my discoveries help me to take full responsibility for my life and help me to create new and positive paths to follow.

I feel my true essence emerge and express itself. Today I am inspired to search within for the strength to continue to freely choose the direction of my life.

*PRESENT MOMENTS*

## I WILL SAVOR EACH MOMENT

Today I will take time to savor the small pleasures the day brings. I will concentrate on small periods of time, present time. I will not get bogged down in past anxieties or apprehensions about the future.

I want to savor this day, to truly dwell in the present—each second, each minute, each hour.

Growing up in a troubled family, I often gave up the present moment to dwell on past hurts and future fears. NO MORE! Today the present is mine, and I will savor it.

*SELF-RESPONSIBILITY*

### I TAKE CHARGE OF
### MY LIFE TODAY

I am a free person, and I assume complete responsibility for my life today. I am pleased with the knowledge that I can freely choose the directions I want my life to take.

I do not blame anyone for where I am today. I make no accusations, I do not find fault with others.

By accepting responsibility in pursuing my direction and my happiness, I begin a healing process. I am free from guilt and free from unhealthy dependence on others. I am free from resentments toward others for somehow "failing" me. I am free to make my own decisions about life today.

Blind, unthinking responsibility for others drains my energy, saps my vigor. But responsibility for myself liberates me and deserves my attention and love.

I take the time today to find out what is most important to me, so that my life will reflect what I believe. I will take charge, full charge of my life today.

*SERENITY*

### I WILL DO WHATEVER I CAN
### TO ENSURE MY SERENITY

My life is calm and orderly. I will allow enough time for myself to do what I need and to get where I am going. Crisis is no longer a condition that I live with.

In my family of origin, crisis was common and made life confused, chaotic. Feelings of anxiety and fear were my constant companions as I grew up in my alcoholic home.

As an adult, I freely leave behind crisis and chaos and choose to be calm and orderly. I will do whatever I can to ensure my serenity and my peace of mind.

I will organize my life to run smoothly. I will eliminate clutter from my life, and I will shun discord and overcomplications. Remembering to think before I act, I will, above all, be kind to myself and ensure serenity by organizing my life and avoiding situations filled with pandemonium and turmoil.

Today I slow down and let serenity flow into my life.

*APPRECIATION*

## I AM APPRECIATED
## AND I APPRECIATE OTHERS

Today I will surround myself with people who value my own worth as well as their own. Even though others might not express their appreciation, still I know that the world was created for my sake. What more personal assurance of my own belonging to the universe can I find than the fact that a divine power has placed me here and arrayed all the bounty and the beauty of the world before me.

I feel appreciated today, not just for what I do, but for who I am. I acknowledge my abilities and talents, as well as the special essence that is me.

Today I leave behind the competitive "you" or "me" from the past. Each of us has a special place in the universe. Knowing this, I can appreciate my friends and colleagues for all that they do and all that they are. Another person's success or achievement does not diminish my own.

This day I am a part of the wonderful exchange of appreciation that makes each person feel needed, wanted and important.

*GIVING*

## I CAN GIVE TO OTHERS
## WITH NO STRINGS ATTACHED

I am changing my definition about what makes a good mother, a good father, a good person. A good person is not a giving machine. I am not expected, nor do I choose to continue to give more than I receive. I don't have to persuade others to like me or to notice me. In my own right, I am likable, lovable, and noticeable.

As a child, I needed much more attention than I received. I grew up with the notion that if I can just give enough, maybe I'll start getting back. This belief is erroneous and destructive for me.

Today I will give when appropriate and when I desire. I will not use giving as a mechanism to coerce others into feeling sorry for me. Giving is lovely when it is given in the spirit of free choice.

Today the motivation for my giving is clean—no strings attached.

*TACT*

## I AM TACTFUL IN MY DEALINGS WITH OTHERS

I have a poised and quiet trust in my ability to meet and handle whatever is before me. I have a self-assurance that comes from the realization of my inner spiritual power and strength.

In my dealings with people today, I am prepared for all situations. I communicate in a tactful, loving way—straightforward and without resentment, sarcasm or bitterness. And I see that when I'm tactful, others feel at ease, feel more trusting and self-confident. Tactfully, I can say what I want to say with patience and understanding.

A situation may seem difficult, a person may seem difficult, but my inner strength enables me to cope tactfully and helpfully. My faith in the spiritual inner strength within myself and others helps me to become a catalyst for healing.

*EXPRESSING LOVE*

### *TODAY I WILL TELL SOMEONE CLOSE TO ME THAT I LOVE THEM*

I can learn to express my love for someone by actions and by words. It is important for me to express my caring for another and yet it might be difficult. Perhaps I may have grown up in a home where I never saw love expressed. Perhaps I allow my fear of rejection stop me from fully expressing myself.

I am learning a new vocabulary of feelings. Learning to be comfortable in sharing deep and intimate emotions is something that will become easier with practice. How do I tell someone that I love them? How do I break through my fear to express all that I feel?

I will begin slowly at first. Learning doesn't happen in an instant, and I won't expect perfection. I take a deep breath, acknowledge my fear—and **then** say what I want to say. I will observe my own feelings and not focus on an expected reaction from my partner.

With experience and practice, I am entering into deeper levels of love.

*SETTING LIMITS*

### *I HAVE A CLEAR, WELL-DEFINED SENSE OF MYSELF*

Today I celebrate my boundaries, I celebrate my clearly-defined sense of self. As I progress in recovery, my fuzzy edges are becoming defined.

In my alcoholic home, it was never clear as to what was my responsibility and what was not. Cause and effect thinking was usually distorted. I felt that I caused events that had nothing to do with me. In the past, my damaged boundaries allowed me to take on others' pain and assume it as my own. It was never clear where I ended and others began.

Today I have a clearly-defined sense of me. I know what feelings are mine and what feelings belong to others. I know what is my responsibility and what is not.

Today I am beginning to establish my limits and say, "No, I won't!" and even, "You can't make me!" I can depend on my feelings and trust my body to establish and maintain clear boundaries.

*PREDICTIONS*

### *I FREE MYSELF FROM OLD PREDICTIONS AND PROPHECIES*

I look at my old programming today, examine the old predictions and the prophecies of doom and gloom, and I erase the tape that plays the self-defeating, shaming messages.

Critical parents and others in my life predicted that I would turn out to be no good, useless or unproductive. These predictions may be showing up in my life as self-fulfilling prophecies. In many situations, there seems to be an unseen parent hovering over my shoulder and whispering, "I told you so."

Today I see that I can change the programming. There is no authority who can predict my success or failure. The only critical parent that exists for me today is the one I carry around in my own head. I am my own best critic, and I will not be harsh and punitive to myself.

I have already surpassed all the predictions made for me by my parents, teachers and close relatives. I predict that I will grow and do well in life.

*PRIDE*

## I FEEL GOOD ABOUT MYSELF TODAY, AND I LIVE MY LIFE WITH PRIDE

Today I will be present at my own life. I will not view my life as a spectator sport, I will take risks, cultivate eccentricity, even live dangerously. In short, I am getting closer to being myself. My life is worth living, and I can be proud of it.

What I do today is important, because I am exchanging a day of life for it. To bring about a healthy self-image, I must assume control of my destiny and become a person who makes things happen.

My life is where this action starts. As I actively start making changes in my life, I will start to feel good about myself. As I express my talents and capabilities, I am allowing the expression of my perfect self. I live my life with pride.

*UNFINISHED BUSINESS*
 *I TAKE CARE OF BUSINESS TODAY*
   Today I release all forms of clutter and confusion from my personal and professional
affairs. At this moment, I declare that I function dynamically with a clear mind, receptive
to fresh thoughts and new opportunities.
   I release myself from all "holding patterns"
of belief. I see a clear distinction between the
way it was in my alcoholic home when I was
growing up, and the way it is today. I live my
life in the NOW, which is my only reality.
   Free from all forms of clutching or hanging
on, I fulfill my obligations with punctuality
and efficiency. With a clear mind, I eliminate
all backlogs of work as I lovingly give myself to
all my tasks. Tranqulity fills my being as I
complete all unfinished business. I experience
release from tension as I attend to matters that
need my attention.

*DECISION-MAKING*

### I MAKE DECISIONS
### WITH CONFIDENCE

I face choices without fear today, for I am confident in my decision-making skills. As I continue to make decisions—fearlessly, boldly—my decision-making proficiency grows.

There was a time in my life when all the decisions I made seemed to be wrong. This was because I was living in the Lose-Lose situation that an alcoholic home creates. Today, I recognize that I am free to make appropriate decisions with confidence.

The more decisions I make, the more accurate I am becoming. From past unwise decisions, I experience growth. When I make the right decisions, I gain increased confidence and freedom to move in any direction at **my** will.

When I am faced with choices, I will not allow the past to paralyze my ability to take responsibility for myself. Today I will write my own story by the decisions that I make.

*HEALTHY THOUGHTS*

### I SILENCE OLD NEGATIVE MESSAGES AND REPLACE THEM WITH HEALTHY THOUGHTS

My beliefs affect my life. When my energy is expended on negative thoughts, I get the same old negative results. I have a very decided part in achieving the changes that I desire. I must silence the negative beliefs that have no bearing on my life today.

If old thoughts of anxiety or shame enter my thinking, I can silence them with soothing voices of my healthy adult self. Self-talk can be a useful tool for me. For positive changes to occur, it is not enough to wish that my life were different. If I don't keep on thinking in accord with the progress I have made, I do not get good results.

Today I will concentrate upon the very things I would like to see taking place in my life. I will not allow old mental habits to erode the changes I desire.

## BUILDING ON MISTAKES

# I ACCEPT MY MISTAKES AND LET THEM CONTRIBUTE TO MY LEARNING AND GROWTH

The price I must pay for any knowledge is to discover it for myself. I must learn my own lessons—I must make my own mistakes. I must pay my own consequences. The knowledge that I gain presents me with a challenge. I can choose to remain where I am and stagnate or I can choose to grow.

My goal is to be able to look at myself and feel good about my achievements and my mistakes. I understand that the choices I have made are neither good nor bad, but wise or unwise. I can neutralize feelings of guilt and shame when I realize that past inadequacies were dependent upon my particular state of awareness at that time.

When I look back at past situations with newly-acquired awareness, I wonder how I could have been so naive or unintelligent. I will treat myself kindly today as I realize that I was not as aware **then** as I am **now.**

Today I accept that my life is, to date, the best that I can accomplish. I will continue to improve as I grow in success and in wisdom.

*HEALTH*

## I EXPECT TO BE HEALTHY

It is God's intention to create a universe that is whole, pure and balanced. So, too, my physical health is an expression of what God intends. The truth is that I am meant to be well and whole.

As a child of an alcoholic, I sometimes tend to ignore my physical needs. Far too often, I pay little attention to health. Today, however, I will examine my habits of living. Whether I am in need of exercise, good nutrition, or medical care, I hereby resolve to take care of my body.

Today I will take a good look at my life and make sure I am not indulging in activities that are not good for me. I want good health, and will be open to change, not defensive about my self-defeating habits. I will work toward my good health, I will make the effort it takes to change, for I expect to be healthy.

*LETTING GO*

### TODAY I LET GO OF THE THINGS I CAN'T CONTROL

The concept of letting go is difficult to grasp. When my home life was chaotic, I tried everything in my power to control what I could. When my home life was rigid, I was taught that to be out of control was disastrous. To conceive of letting go of things over which I have no control sounds good—but what does it mean?

To let go and let God take over doesn't mean I give up. Rather, it means that I do the best I can. It means that I don't have to control the outcome of every event. Letting go is a positive act of faith. It is releasing the idea that I must carry the whole load and the whole weight of responsibility for anyone or anything.

I feel a great sense of relief in knowing that I have only to do my part, to take responsibility for my own actions. I take it easy today and relax my hold on the fine art of never giving up. Trusting and relaxed, I surrender.

*GOOD JUDGMENT*

### I MAKE WISE CHOICES AND
### I HAVE GOOD JUDGMENT

I listen to my inner wisdom for help in all situations. I allow my inner wisdom to let me know what I need to do.

When there is a flow between my head and my heart, I make wise decisions. But I must open myself more fully to the voice of my inner wisdom, I must quiet the noise and clamor within, so that my inner wisdom can be heard.

Jane Bradford Thurber wrote:

> Dear God,
> Help me to be still and know
> That you are there
> I was making so much noise
> That I couldn't hear you.

Each day I increase my ability to act in ways that promote good and healthy results. I do not allow my fear of what others might think pressure me into acting against my own better judgment.

Today I handle my affairs wisely and with confidence.

*SUCCESS*

### TODAY I APPROACH ALL OF MY PROJECTS WITH CONFIDENCE

I deserve to live this day triumphantly. Today I choose to experience joy as I keep my heart and mind open to wonderful experiences.

I approach all projects today with confidence and faith in my success. Whether a small project or a great undertaking, I will finish each task and know my success is assured. I will silence all remarks of failure and realize that these are voices from the past. They have no bearing on my life today.

I have the ability, as a spiritual being, to assume control over my life. Within me exists Divine potential to meet each day joyously with faith in my success.

*LOVING AND BEING LOVED*

### *I AM FREE TO LOVE AND BE LOVED*

Today I announce my readiness to attract loving experiences into my life. I desire it, I deserve it, and I am able to accept it.

I release all beliefs that keep these experiences from me. Thoughts of competition, jealously or rejection have no place in my consciousness today. Past or present hurts do not have the power to exclude me from the Divine activity of Love. I release all people in my life from the burden of having to make me feel securely loved. I am liberated from false needs to defend myself.

When I remove my armor, people feel safe in my presence and are free to love me. I am free to love. This freedom is communicated to all those around me.

Today I celebrate my expanding capacity to love and be loved.

*INNER VOICE*

## MY INTUITION IS MY GUIDE

I now trust my intuition and let it guide me in enhancing every area of my life. Today I will pay attention to the voice inside, my intuitive self. I will take time to listen, to evaluate and to act appropriately.

My intuition is a gift that bestows knowledge on me when I need it. Right ideas are always available—waiting in my consciousness to be used for my good.

In my alcoholic home, I often silenced my inner voice. As a child, my intuition kept me safe and at the same time urged me to express myself. In adulthood, I will no longer live with this double bind.

Today I welcome my inner knowing and listen attentively. Today I appreciate the creative ideas my intuition brings.

*RISK*

## WONDERFUL CHOICES ARE
## AVAILABLE TO ME

Today I set aside customary patterns and enter the arena of discovery. Today I see a wealth of options that are available to me. I will release the richness of my imagination and explore behaviors and thoughts which I never dreamed possible.

Today I chart my course with confidence and courage. I know that my Higher Power will inspire my ideas and protect me in carrying them out. This day I offer myself a banquet of experiences. I will accept the challenge and risk experimentation and investigation into new ways of being. Unexpected surprises await me as I anticipate only good.

*REJUVENATION*

## I HAVE A NEW AND ABIDING WARMTH IN MY SOUL

The harsh winter winds still call attention to themselves, though winter is coming to a close. I am mindful of all the unpleasant aspects of this most unfriendly of seasons. Some memories of my unhappy childhood still linger within me, blowing icy blasts through my soul. I am aware of these currents, just as I am aware of the chill in the world around me.

There is no longer a need to struggle against these elements, for I have a new and abiding warmth in my soul. I am as unique and important to life's scheme as each snowflake. I am as content and patient as the roots of the great trees in the forest are, and I know full well that the warmth, sunshine and fresh breezes of spring will rejuvenate me.

Today I am aware of the abiding warmth and love in my soul patiently awaiting the coming of spring.

*SURVIVAL*

## I AM IN CHARGE AGAIN

Today I notice a change as I become willing to let go of my pain. Pain will still exist for me, but letting go means that I can bear my pain without the fear that I will be absorbed or consumed by it.

Today I no longer identify myself solely with my pain. I enter this day with a deep knowing that there is more to life than the pain I own. I know now that my pain is truly mine. I am no longer possessed or controlled by it. My anxiety dissolves as I realize that my pain will not kill me.

Today I know that I WILL survive. All the torn pieces of me are coming together as I acknowledge my own healing power. My pain is no longer in charge of me.

Today I am once again in charge.

*CALMNESS*

### I STILL MY THOUGHTS AND SEARCH FOR THAT QUIET PLACE WITHIN ME

At this moment I still the anxieties of my hurried thinking and center on that quiet place within me. In this quiet place, great spiritual ideas are revealed. I accept them and follow through on them. I take this moment to rest from my usual concerns and take a deep breath and fill my spirit with peace.

For the moment, I relax from all fear, worry, and doubt. In this calm peace, I find a healing power that sets my consciousness free to create positive beliefs and feelings. This calmness will prevail throughout my day.

I begin this day knowing that all negative interference in my thoughts is dissolved. I am at one with the love of God and this love will spill over into my relationships, my business affairs, my health and my well-being.

*PLAY*

### TODAY I COAX THE CHILD
### OUT OF MY SOUL

I take delight in play today, knowing that I have a right to pursue pleasurable activities. I deserve to enjoy myself in a non-destructive way. I will no longer become so focused on outside activities that I ignore my own need for fun and laughter. I will not be over-responsible for others and under-responsible for myself.

I can play and have fun without becoming overwhelmed with guilt or anxiety. I can pursue people and situations where I can coax the delightful "child" out of my soul. Today I will separate myself from my responsibilities and know that I am not defined only by what I do.

Today I invite my child to play. Whether outrageous, adorable, nasty or naughty. I bless my child self and give it love.

*NEEDS*

## I AM THE ONLY EXPERT
## ON WHAT I NEED

I base my decisions on my needs today. I am learning to be sensitive to the changes I'm going through in recovery. I'm learning to be flexible with my new needs and patterns. What was appropriate for me yesterday may no longer work in my life now.

I feel free to experiment with new styles of behaving, thinking and feelings. The changes I am going through may not be permanent. I know only that if these changes are helpful now, I will use them.

As I learn about myself, I test and question my old patterns, my old values. I evaluate what feels good and what does not. Since I am the only expert on what feels good to me, I will base my decisions on **my needs.**

Today I treat myself with kindness and patience.

*FEELINGS*

### MY EMOTIONAL LIFE IS A UNIQUE EXPRESSION OF ME

All of my feelings are important. I am slowly losing fear of my own emotions. This fear of expressing my feelings has caused me to repress or deny them. I know that if I hold to this pattern, my body will eventually scream— even if I do not. I will no longer treat myself unkindly.

In the past, I might have judged my feelings harshly. I no longer believe that my anger, sadness or caring caused the alcoholism in my family. I will not deprive myself of an emotional life because of false beliefs.

My emotional life is unique, and a unique feeling pattern is emerging as I learn free expression.

*JUDGMENT*

## MY JUDGMENT IS SOUND
## AS I UTILIZE MY INNER WISDOM

I have good judgment in handling my thoughts and emotions today. I eliminate all fear and all false imaginations that cause me anxiety.

The judgments and perceptions of others do not disturb my peace of mind today. I am the authority over my experiences.

This day I am anchored in truth.

I will no longer place unconditional trust in people or beliefs that are destructive for me. I can protect myself by listening to my feelings. My inner wisdom will provide me with all the guidance I need.

Today I use my judgment and clear my consciousness of negative ideas, situations and people.

*UNFINISHED BUSINESS*

## I EMBARK UPON THIS DAY WITH MY MENTAL HOUSE IN ORDER

Today is a day for spring cleaning. It is the time, after a long winter, to open my mind and let in fresh ideas and release stale thoughts. I rummage through thoughts and emotions, and I notice unfinished business clinging like cobwebs in the corners of my mind.

I sweep the cobwebs and the dust away. I light up my consciousness and illuminate the nooks and crannies where old useless fears are stored.

I rid myself of bitterness, I discard shabby resentments and other outmoded patterns of behavior that I no longer need. I cleanse away the grime, the self-criticism and blame. I cleanse away the shame. I let in fresh air, fresh thoughts, and I let in the light.

Uncluttered, I feel a brightness and a clarity of purpose. The scent of springtime and new beginnings permeate the air. My house is in order and I am ready to start this day.

*DISCOVERY*

# I AM ON A JOURNEY TO DISCOVER THE STRONG INNER ME

I will open myself to risk and to surprise. Like all journeys, the quest for self-knowledge can bring strength and illumination.

I have confidence. I will accept both my power and my needs. I will recognize that my strength comes from caring and nurturing myself, and from caring and nurturing others. I will reflect on those I love and know that I, too, am loved. I bask in the warmth of this knowledge.

I have needs, and I am an important person. I will not be diminished, but will grow deep, take root, and cultivate power. As I search, I will discover and revel in the many facets of my inner strength.

*CLARITY*

## CLARITY IS ALWAYS
## WITHIN MY REACH

My thinking is simplified today as I center my attention on my inner voice. So often in my alcoholic home, the environment was chaotic and complicated. As a child, I seemed to be always caught up in cross-currents of confusion. As an adult, my thinking sometimes becomes muddled and I have trouble making decisions.

I have the ability to simplify my thinking. I can pause and take time to look over the pros and cons of a decision and not become overwhelmed.

When I am called upon to make a decision, I will quiet my thoughts and align myself with divine order. I will listen to my inner voice as I let my Higher Power guide and direct my thinking.

Clarity is available to me and order is already established. I have only to tune in and listen.

*LAUGHTER*

### I REJOICE IN MY LAUGHTER

Laughter is a vital part of life, born in a baby's smile. I am alive with delight. As I continue to recover, I am more aware of the healing that laughter brings. Laughter is one of God's gifts to lighten the heart. I accept and reflect happiness and see it appearing everywhere.

Humor is an integral part of life, and I rejoice in the manifestation of it. Laughter is the music of my soul and my spirit. Today I connect my head and my heart with the complete release that laughter brings.

*MOTIVATION*

### I AM MOTIVATED
### TO PURSUE MY GOAL

Today I will pursue my goals and set my sights towards motivating myself. There is no need for me to lead an empty, unfulfilled life. If I am not sure where I am going, I will take the time to ask God for light and inspiration.

What is my sincere desire in life? Have I settled for a day-to-day existence that offers comfort and security, but does not challenge me? Perhaps for the first time in my life, I will pursue what **I** desire. **I** will set **my** goals, not based upon anyone's opinion of me.

Today I feel motivated to experience life to its fullest. I realize that each situation I encounter can only be for my Higher Education. I press forward, I do not give up or become discouraged.

I have the will and the motivation to pursue that which I desire.

*HIGHER POWER*

### I WILL STEP ASIDE AND
### LET GOD TAKE OVER

Today I will stand aside and let the Higher Power work through me. I will no longer try to block my Higher Power by my own efforts. Today I will put my ego in the background and allow my inner voice to show me the way.

I will not interfere with the working of God's spirit in me and through me.

Sometimes my mind gets so cluttered that I feel like a rubber ball—bouncing with no direction. When I feel this way, perhaps I am running from something I must do—look at—or feel. I know there is a direction for me, if I can only get quiet enough to listen.

Today I affirm my courage to look inward, to seek out that internal and eternal source of wisdom. Today I will not get in my way.

*OPTIMISM*

## I MEET LIFE'S CHALLENGES OPTIMISTICALLY

Today I am optimistic about the experiences and people that come into my life. I will view all encounters as opportunities to expand my awareness. I am not threatened by people or by situations. Challenges only serve to stir up the gifts within me; they are for my highest good.

With this trust, this optimism, I cannot be victimized by any situation. I will only be energized. I bless my challenges, for they provide me with the opportunities to exercise myself.

Optimism enables me to welcome the changes that occur in my life. When I anticipate change with dread and fear, I only block myself from going forward. Change gives me the gift of growth. I appreciate my freedom to become myself and the challenges that enable me to actualize my potential.

*PRACTICE*

## I WILL BEGIN TODAY TO PUT INTO PRACTICE MY NEW LEARNINGS

Knowledge has power only when it is used. Now that I possess all kinds of information about my life, how am I using it? Perhaps I have read many books and countless articles, or attended lectures concerning the source of my problems.

Am I putting this information to good use, or am I simply accumulating knowledge? If I am still experiencing inner discomfort or pain, perhaps this is a reminder that I must put some ideas into action.

Today I recognize that it is better to try one good idea than to accumulate a hundred and not practice them. It is important for me to move from theory into personal experience. All the information is of no benefit to me until I take a risk and prove to myself that I can take the first step.

Within me is an unlimited potential to be all that I desire. I will begin to put into practice what I have learned.

*INTIMACY*

## I AM ATTRACTED TO PEOPLE WHO ARE AVAILABLE FOR INTIMACY

New territory is opening to me as I acquaint myself with my feelings and beliefs. I am open to experimenting with new behavior as I release the shackles of my past programming.

Being attracted to someone I cannot have is safe. This becomes harmful for me only when I make this a way of life. If I wish to grow, I must be willing to look at my fear of intimacy with a real person in the here and now. It is no longer satisfying for me to drift in a cloud of self-deception.

Day by day, I am getting ready to accept the challenges of intimacy. I have turned the bright lights on the dark mechanical patterns of my past. With my deepening self-awareness, I deserve a relationship that is attainable.

*TIMING*

### I CULTIVATE PATIENCE AND ALLOW SOLUTIONS TO COME AT THEIR OWN PACE

Today I will not rush toward solutions. There is a proper time for everything and I must learn to respect the flow of events and my own sense of timing. I must learn patience. When I rush into something before I'm prepared, or before conditions are right, I usually wish later that I would have listened to myself. Often I get impatient, and I'm tempted to do everything all at once, instead of taking it easy, a little at a time.

Today I will have patience; I will delay action until I feel that I am doing the right thing at the right time. By cultivating balance and timing, I can be more effective.

I will silence the voices in my mind that push me to act before thinking. I know that real solutions will come when I patiently listen to my own emotional and intellectual processes.

*DESTINY*

### I AM DESTINED TO EXPERIENCE
### HAPPINESS AND JOY

I was created to be happy. I will turn off all the critical voices that tell me otherwise. I deserve happiness. Nothing harmful will happen to me if I am happy, and I will organize my life so that I can make happiness possible. I will not live by the double standard of professing to desire happiness and undermining my happiness by my actions.

Martyrdom and self-sacrifice have no place in my life. I do not have to re-create the life story of my alcoholic home. In love relationships, I will not choose a partner in suffering. I am not looking for a person who will reject me, let me down or abandon me.

I am a person who is destined to be happy. I am attracted to partners with whom I can clearly experience happiness and joy.

CREATIVITY

### I AM USING MY CREATIVITY TO BECOME THE BEST THAT I CAN BE

I will use my creativity and imagination in solving my own problems. I will trust in my own mental, emotional and spiritual powers to resolve my concerns. In this way, I will release my creativity.

I will not be afraid to speculate—to let my mind find new channels for change, even if that seems impossible. I am discovering new realities about myself because I am daring to think differently.

I can use the same freedom of imagination to come up with new ideas for myself. I am a creative person who is involved in an exciting project—my self-transformation.

I will use all of my resources and trust my inherent ability to move toward my utmost good.

*NEW BEGINNINGS—FIRST DAY OF SPRING*

### I WILL BEGIN TODAY WITH HOPEFUL ATTITUDES AND A SENSE OF RENEWAL

In the morning when I arise, I will begin life anew. I approach this day with a fresh outlook: Today does not need to be a rerun, nor does it need to be a stale repetition of yesterday's unhappiness. Yesterday's stresses belong to yesterday.

I trust my Higher Power to guide me toward letting go of all that I cannot control. I see that my life stresses stem from many events I cannot control, and from my automatic reactions to decisions made by others.

Today I start again, fresh, renewed. I will separate from yesterday's burdens and I will allow positive energy to flow through me as I greet the day with clear thoughts and no fears.

*LOVE AND HARMONY*

## I AM IN CHARGE OF MY LIFE— I CHOOSE TO EXPERIENCE LOVE AND HARMONY

I am the one in charge of my every experience. It is my life-long responsibility to take charge of all that I am. I do this with delightful anticipation, knowing that I possess the power and strength to create a healthy existence.

The messages that I give myself today will be clear, positive and definite. I will be sure that these messages are received by putting them into action.

Critical or judgmental voices play no part in my thinking as I listen to my inner wisdom. I will not permit any voice, within or without, to sway me from my chosen path of health, love, and wholeness.

I am the Chairman of my Board. I am in charge of my life always, and I write my own agenda. Inner dissension and disruption will be squelched, as I conduct my life in balance and harmony.

*UNIQUENESS*

## *I VALUE WHAT IS UNIQUE IN ME*

I value my own specialness, and I dare to reveal it. Since the universe expresses itself through the differences in all of creation, I choose to acknowledge my own uniqueness. My inner self speaks through the nonconformity that I am. Today I applaud nonconformity and the differences within my life.

I am free of the need to please others or to conform to what they are. When I am true to myself, I easily and lovingly express my own opinions and beliefs without fear of rejection. My self worth is not on the line when I recognize the uniqueness in myself and others. I do not have to agree with everyone, and everyone does not have to agree with me. Belief in my differentness allows me to understand those who do not understand me.

I praise my uniquenss and wear it proudly.

*SELFISHNESS*

# I HAVE MY NEEDS,
# MY WANTS, MY VALUES

It is perfectly all right for me to be selfish. Recovery means that I am honoring my needs, my wants and my values. In short, I am honoring my own life. I have the courage to stand by my convictions and fight for my own happiness.

As a child, I was taught that selfishness was a dirty word. In an alcoholic environment, it is not acceptable to concentrate on your own needs.

Today, however, I realize that unless I honor my own interests, I will not survive. I am learning that the self is to be celebrated—not denied, abandoned or sacrificed. Even in the most intimate and loving relationships, I still need to respect my own needs and wants. If I don't, I will lose myself and eventually lose the relationship.

I am learning to be selfish in the healthiest sense of the word.

*HERE AND NOW*

## AS I EXPAND MY AWARENESS, EACH MOMENT IS RICH

I know that I can improve my life. I can do so day by day and enjoy each moment. As each moment unfolds, I realize that I am, right now, the best that I can be. God gave me this life to live and the potential to be happy in it. It is completely up to me to enjoy being who and what I am. As I gradually let go of my troubled past, I become more aware of how wonderful it is to be me.

For at least these few moments, I will clear away the cobwebs of fear, depression and anxiety from my consciousness. I will let the strong currents of love flow through me, sweeping away all thought of limitation or critical disapproval. I am left only with a sense of peace and happiness. My every moment today will be filled with a never-ending variety of experiences, which will expand my joy of living.

*RECEIVING GIFTS*

### *I AM LEARNING TO RECEIVE— I AM READY TO ACCEPT MY GOOD*

I am teaching myself to be a willing, gracious receiver. Learning how to accept good is an all-important task. When someone gives me something, I will receive it graciously and not negate the gift by saying, "Oh, you shouldn't have done that!"

Neither will I avoid the enjoyment of receiving by immediately calculating what to give the giver in return.

Part of learning how to receive is accepting myself as worthy. I will begin to receive abundance when I mentally accept that I am deserving of unlimited good. If I resist or reject this belief, I will not avail myself of life's bountiful gifts.

The next time I am given a gift, I will not scrutinize, analyze or wonder what strings are attached. These are old patterns, based on old fears. I know that life does not give only to those who deserve. Life gives only to those who know they deserve.

*HERE AND NOW*
### I CHOOSE TO LIVE FULLY IN THE PRESENT

Today I choose to start fresh, because today is all that I have. My present world is created out of my present beliefs. I will not immobilize myself by continuing to blame my present experience on my past. Yesterday has very little to do with today unless I am guided by yesterday's beliefs.

Only I can choose what I wish to think and feel today. I am learning how to function in a creative, positive way. This means that I am letting go of self-defeating patterns from the past. I am giving myself a healthy evaluation based on self-love. I do not carry the old remarks and shaming comments with me into the future. Who I am—is who I am TODAY.

The power exists within me to change my life—and so I will.

*CHOICES*

## *MY LIFE IS SHAPED BY MY CHOICES*

My decisions are like statements of my identity. My choices reflect the core of my being. Every decision I make embodies my self concept and my view of the world.

Today I am aware that choices are not isolated events on the periphery of my life. Choices **are** my life.

Making good decisions means paying attention to what I think and what I feel. It is when I take notice of my beliefs and emotions that I can draw on the vital wisdom that I possess. Today I will become conscious of my motivations. I will learn what beliefs propel me toward or away from what I truly desire.

Guided by my Higher Power and spiritual awareness, I will make choices today that grow out of awareness and sensitivity to my deepest needs.

*SELF-PITY*

### I FACE MY EMOTIONS AND EXPERIENCE THEM FREELY

I can talk about my pain and not fear that I am overdoing it, or that people will pity me. I will not disown myself from my pain; neither will I indulge in self-pity. There is a distinct difference between acknowledging pain and blaming others for it.

I will not cling to my pain as an excuse for inactivity, nor will I complain about my pain while seeking to avoid it.

Talking about my uncomfortable feelings can be therapeutic and relieving. It requires courage and honesty, and it is not an exercise in self-indulgence. When I tell someone how I'm feeling, I am taking responsibility for my awareness. I enter the realm of self-pity when I make no effort to deal with my suffering or to understand it. I am indulging in self-pity when I abandon responsibility for my feelings and surrender to passivity.

I see that when I face my emotions and experience them freely, I take a big step toward recovery. Today I face my pain, and I move through it.

*CONTROL*

## *TODAY I FEEL A STRONG SENSE OF SELF-DETERMINATION*

I have a sense of self-determination when I am clear about what is important to me. I have control over my life when I set goals and see that I am working toward those goals by gathering the knowledge and the skills necessary to achieve them.

The essence of feeling in control of my life comes from my determination, motivation and knowledge. I also know that in times of crisis, my inner strength is tested.

I will not spend my time trying to manage other people and events. Neither will I deceive myself by believing that I am in charge when I am controlled by how other people respond to me.

I am learning lessons daily about my inner strengths and my self-determination. I have weathered the storm of growing up in an alcoholic family. I have learned from this experience and have tapped the depth of my self-knowledge.

Today I am taking control of my life by learning the skills necessary for living a healthy, productive life.

*APPRECIATION*

### I HAVE A NEW VISION OF MYSELF AND THE WORLD TODAY

Today I see the world differently by changing my mind about what I want to see. I am not a victim of the world.

What I see in the world is a projection—an outpicturing—of what I have first seen in my own mind. I am co-creator of my reality, not a passive receiver, not a blank sheet of paper that life writes upon.

I am not a victim of life. I no longer label myself a victim—I am a survivor. I am no longer victimized by my thoughts and feelings or attitudes. What I choose to accept is a consciousness of love and strength; and, as co-creator of my reality, I see the world afresh.

I now accept my new vision of myself and the world.

*FREEDOM*

### I FEEL A BOUNDLESS FREEDOM

I am not bound by anything, and I can express freedom now. I do not have to wait until next week or next month to feel free. I do not have to wait until challenges are removed from my life.

I can be free now. Today I sense unerringly that freedom begins within my mind.

Rich possibilities stretch in a panorama before me, inviting me onward and upward. Today I visualize my disappointments vanishing like mist before the morning sun.

*COURAGE*

### *I HAVE THE COURAGE TO EMERGE FROM SECRECY*

The rule of silence is broken ... I am no longer isolated.

I will no longer live in secrecy. I will no longer deny the connection between my current pain and my experiences in my alcoholic family. The tremendous energy that I have used to keep the rule of silence is now relinquished. I feel relieved.

The wall of isolation I have built around myself crumbles as I realize that I am not alone. There are millions of people who, like myself, have had the courage to speak out.

I am beginning to experience long-hidden emotions as I enter into my healing process. I will be gentle and patient with myself and not rush through my recovery. It is not my responsibility to save my family or to force them to acknowledge the problem.

The silence is broken—a new beginning is available as I affirm My Courage.

*JOY*

## *I FEEL STRESS-FREE TODAY AND LIVE IN JOYOUS EXISTENCE*

Today I turn to that quiet place within me and find ever-present renewal, strength and refreshment. I feel no pressure or stress. I have an inner calm. I am restored, and I live in joyous existence.

Strain and pressure are made by man, but they need not belong in my world.

Today I am relaxed and at ease around others. I feel the quiet strength of my Higher Power and I allow the joy of serenity to enfold me.

## CHOICEMAKING

### *I AM AN EXPERT SAILOR—I WILL CHART MY COURSE, SET MY SAILS AND REACH MY GOALS*

A sailboat on the high seas is at the mercy of the waves, the currents, the winds and the weather. The waves can be high, the currents can be strong, the winds can be fierce and the weather unpredictable. Yet an expert sailor can set a course and adjust the sails so that the boat reaches the desired destination.

A child of an alcoholic, I am well aware of life's "high winds" and unpredictable weather. I have spent my energies trying to fight the strong currents and the pounding waves, and I have become exhausted and discouraged. It is through recovery that I become an expert sailor. Instead of being destroyed by the events in my life, I too can adjust my sails and allow strong winds to help me reach my destination.

The powerful choices I make determine how I steer my life. When I refuse to make healthy choices, I wander off course and become overwhelmed by life's circumstances. Yes, I am powerless over the elements, but not impotent.

I take this moment to appreciate my God-given ability to steer my life in desirable ways. No matter what faces me, my choices can lead me to a better place.

(93)

*FORGIVENESS*

## I FORGIVE MYSELF AND OTHERS WHO HAVE HURT ME

I can forgive and let go.

I cannot forget the past of the family I was raised in. But I **can** learn from my experiences and not repeat them if I choose.

Today I know that only through forgiveness can I release my guilt and fear. Forgiving myself will be complete when I can forgive others.

Today I choose to let go of resentment. I no longer allow these emotions to fester inside of me.

I experience new freedom today as I forgive myself and others who have hurt me.

*LOVE*

## TODAY I RADIATE A SPIRIT OF LOVE, JOY AND HAPPINESS

I radiate a spirit of love, joy and happiness. To radiate love is to become a magnet for good. To radiate love is to overcome loneliness. Throughout the day, I keep in mind that I am a radiating center of Divine Love. It will make a difference in my day; it will make a difference in the way other see me and in the way I feel about myself.

Today I am centered, grounded in love, and I attract good, in delightful ways.

*PATIENCE*

## I HAVE PATIENCE NOW AND KNOW THAT GOOD THINGS WILL COME INTO MY LIFE

Today I release my expectations that everything must improve at this moment. Good things are now coming into my life. Fuller and healthier relationships are possible, but they do take time. Nurturing a meaningful relationship takes patience.

Just as plants need cultivation to grow, so do relationships. I have faith that the relationships I nurture and cultivate will surely bloom.

Today I have a quiet optimism and faith in the good things coming into my life, and I have patience with myself and with others as I move toward self-fulfillment.

*CREATIVITY*

### I TAKE GREAT PLEASURE IN MY TALENTS AND CREATIVITY

I have unique gifts to share, gifts which are mine alone. I have talent and creativity, and I take great satisfaction and pleasure in realizing my potential for growth.

I am not limited in my talents or creativity. In living my creative self, I have much to offer, much to give. And by doing so, I realize new joy in my ever-expanding self-fulfillment.

As I increasingly find fulfillment in recovery, I see my unique gifts accepted and appreciated by all those around me. I am valued by friends and colleagues as I continue to grow and change.

Today I acknowledge that in living my creative self, I find the satisfaction for which my soul longs.

*HIGHER POWER*

## I HAVE FAITH IN MY HIGHER POWER TO FIX THE "FAULTY PICTURE" IN MY LIFE

*"Please Stand By ... You Are Receiving a Faulty Picture"*

Today I understand there are some things I cannot fix by will power or sheer effort. In my healing process, I have come to understand that there are unhappy or unpleasant situations in life for which I don't have solutions. I take pleasure and comfort from the knowledge that if I release the situation it will be adjusted by powers other than my own.

In my alcoholic family, I felt the need to solve problems that arose with my other family members. I thought it was in my power to fix the problem as quickly as possible.

Now I realize that there are times when I cannot adjust the "faulty picture," and I accept that all I have to do is wait until the "picture" clears.

Today I affirm the right to just "stand by" and let the faulty picture I am receiving be cleared by a Higher Power.

*LETTING GO*

### TODAY I BID GOODBYE
### TO THE PAST

I take advantage of this day to free myself from the bondage of unhealthy patterns I have learned. I release the past, knowing that its events and experiences have served the purpose, even at the most difficult moments.

I dwell in the present. I cannot escape the past, but I do not carry it with me as I move through recovery. I do not let old habits and emotions from the past color my life today.

Today I will not dwell on the past. I free myself to face this new day with a positive attitude and constructive thoughts.

The past is over, the now is new, fresh and limitless. I welcome it with joyous expectancy.

*LIMITS*

## I AFFIRM MY RIGHT
## TO MAKE DECISIONS

I am learning to set new limits for myself. I see myself as valuable and worthwhile. I treat myself well, and I set limits for myself that are realistic and appropriate.

No longer do I seek approval by going that "extra mile." I will not delay in establishing boundaries for myself. It is important for me to pay attention to my feelings and to learn to say "No!"

My responsibility is to be clear about what I will or will not tolerate. I have every right to exist, to feel what I feel, and to take care of myself by setting limits that are right for me.

Today I affirm my right to decide what I will and will not do.

*HEALING*

## TODAY I ACKNOWLEDGE A DEEP RESPECT FOR MY OWN HEALING PROCESS

Recovery takes time. I will be patient with my healing.

I will not cheat myself of the necessary time it takes to go through my own grief. Knowing that the only way to get through my pain is to go through it, I will not become impatient.

To pretend that I have never experienced real despair is to sabotage myself. I will not participate in emotional dishonesty. I am assured that the strength I need to get through my pain is already within me. I will not ignore my emotions.

Today I entrust myself to God, with a sure knowledge that my healing is now taking place.

*DREAMS*

## TODAY I HAVE THE COURAGE TO KEEP MY DREAMS ALIVE

Keeping my dreams alive is important to me. If one dream dies, I know I must search deeply inside for the glimmer of another.

I have felt betrayed before by dreams that never had a chance, by relationships that have failed and by parents that disappointed me. Even the dreams that have failed played an important part in my life, and I will nurture the spark within me that keeps my dreams alive.

Every lovely reality was someone's dream that was loved into being. Today I will affirm my courage to dream again.

*TRUTH*

### TODAY I SPEAK THE TRUTH IN MY RELATIONSHIPS

When I speak the truth, I am powerful. Just as I am in search of the truth, so will truth manifest itself through my words.

Today, as an adult, I see that old behavior patterns of lying are no longer of use to me. I don't need the child's shield of lying to protect myself. I am keenly aware of my commitment to speak the truth. I do so with kindness and compassion for myself.

The Divine Spirit within me is pure—there is no shame. When I live, speak and feel the truth, I am pure, free, and one with the universe.

I speak truth today, and I am Truth.

*ACCEPTANCE*

## I AM AWARE OF
## TOTAL SELF-ACCEPTANCE

Each day gives me a new opportunity to express the perfection which is within me. With this realization in mind, I bless every individual that I encounter.

I now release all old negative images and refuse to give them any power. They are burdensome and have no place in my life.

Today I replace these old images with perfect acceptance of all that I am.

*HARMONY*

## MY MIND IS AT PEACE

At this moment I am quieting turbulent thoughts and allowing peace to fill my consciousness. I know there is power in a peaceful frame of mind. I do not need to become dependent upon people or things for contentment. All the peace I need exists within me.

It does me no good to allow myself to become focused on anxiety and fear. I acknowledge these emotions and let them pass. In their place, I allow harmony and balance to fill my consciousness.

When my mind is at peace I think clearly and correctly. When my mind is at peace, order is restored, and an overall vision of good exists.

Today I feel my inner strength and power as I let peace fill my consciousness. I am centered in harmony as I bring peace to every relationship.

*BEGINNINGS*

### I BEGIN ANEW

Today can be a turning point, the beginning of a bright new life. It is never too late to begin again. I will make efforts today to set matters straight in my life.

It is not too late for me to make amends, to forgive and let go. I smile as I imagine the possibilities that lie before me.

Today I will stretch my thinking and feeling as I test out new ways of behaving, new ways of expressing myself. I take risks confidently, knowing that I don't have to change everything overnight. It's not too late for me to relieve every burden and enter this day with a new spirit.

*CONTROL*

## TODAY I TAKE CONTROL OF MY AFFAIRS

I have the certain knowledge that I can control my thoughts and feelings. I am not compelled to respond today with the same emotions I had as a child growing up in an alcoholic home.

If I sense negative thoughts or self-defeating behaviors beginning to take hold, or if I feel inferior or inadequate, I know that I need to assert my control. I need to change my perceptions.

As I open my mind to my Higher Power, knowing that I am not bound by any negative thought or condition. I have the wisdom and the strength to say "No!" to unwanted thoughts.

I **can** take control of my life. I can be free and happy as God wants me to be.

*TRUST*

### *I TRUST MY HIGHER POWER TO BRING ABOUT THE PERFECT FULFILLMENT OF GOOD*

Today I relax the tight grip I have on my thoughts and attitudes. I ease up, secure in the knowledge that no disasters will happen if I relax my vigilance. I release all matters to God's Divine Plan for me.

At times I might find it difficult to know how to handle a particular situation, but right answers always come when I acknowledge that my Higher Power is at work.

Today I offer up my fears, my doubts and my feelings of insecurity. I let them go in the sure realization that God's good is unfolding for me in Divine order and Divine timing.

*PARENTING*

## I AM A CONSISTENT, LOVING PARENT

Today I affirm my ability to parent in a way that enhances self-esteem. I have learned from the experiences of my childhood and I don't have to repeat the patterns from my alcoholic home. My children receive my love in a healthy, loving way. I will deliver clear messages that not only tell my children that they are important, but that will also give them guidance in their behavior. I will avoid giving messages that invite my children to fail.

Today I will honor my children by showing that I care enough to set limits for them. I can discipline with respect and with love. If I need help with my parenting, I will not be defensive and full of denial. If I need help, I will get it. If I need to improve my parenting, I can do it.

Today I validate my parenting skills. I appreciate my accomplishments and I accept my mistakes.

*CONSCIOUSNESS*

### *I FEEL FULLY AWAKE AND ALIVE TODAY*

I open my eyes to the many different shades of green in nature. I listen and detect small silences and a wide range of familiar tones in the voices of strangers. I am alert to nuances of taste and smell. I close my eyes and touch a tree trunk and let it instruct me in the meaning of texture.

I will not sleepwalk through life. There have been times in the past when I was not aware of my destructive conditioning. I functioned as a robot and life itself seemed dull and mechanical. But now I am ridding myself of old patterns and old conditioning.

In recovery, I live in the present, in the now. All creation takes place in the present—it's all happening right this instant. Fully conscious and aware, I am attuned to the marvelous organic complexity of life.

Today I feel exhilarated—alive and fully aware. I take the opportunity to be fully conscious. I embrace the opportunity to experience life to its fullest.

*SOLITUDE*

## I EXPERIENCE SOLITUDE WITH CALMNESS AND PEACE

I have no fear of being alone today. I greet solitude as I'd greet an old friend, with warmth and a smile. In solitude I have a respite, a time for calmness and peace, a time for communing deeply with my Higher Power.

Growing up in an alcoholic home, I was afraid of being alone. I dreaded isolation and abandonment. There have been times, as an adult, when I continued in bad relationships rather than be left with loneliness and isolation.

Today, I can be alone but not lonely. I do not shun others; I find time for others—many others in my life, who care for me and support me in my recovery. I need time to myself, when I can be serene, comtemplative and available to wisdom.

Today I give myself time to be alone, and I am calm and relaxed in my quiet solitude.

*AFFECTION*

### I CAN GET HEALTHY
### AFFECTION TODAY

Today I can relax in my relationships with others and get the warmth and affection I need. I am a whole person, whether or not I am in a relationship. In my desire for affection, I am nether greedy nor insatiable.

Affection does not mean salvation. I do not believe that affection or love from another will solve all of my problems.

I will not "wheel and deal" to get the affection that I need. I want to have relationships where I don't have to perform or give up my power to have my needs met. I will not **buy** affection at any cost. I declare myself unwilling to sell my soul, my body or my identity.

Today I possess a deep knowing that I can maintain my sense of self, and still get the affection I need and deserve.

*FRIEND*

## I AM A FRIEND TO MYSELF

Today I am on my own side. I choose to befriend myself and be on my own team, which means that I will not focus my energies today on judging, criticizing, or demeaning myself in any way. It is my responsibility to teach others how to treat me by the way I treat myself.

When I put these words into action, it means that I don't have to constantly point out my faults to myself and to others around me. When I am for me, it means that I will not create my own anxiety by giving myself negative messages. I will not be an enemy to myself.

Today I affirm that "I" will always be **with** me and **for** me.

*HELPER SYNDROME*

### *I RESIST THE IMPULSE TO BE A "GOOD" HELPER*

I don't have to take care of people by thinking for them.

Intimacy is not about helping people do things right, but rather being supportive and on their side. Today I will resist the urge to do a "little lecturing" to those I care about.

I do not have to be a continual fountain of good sense, advice and infinite wisdom. Intimacy means I can simply **be** with someone. I don't have to take care of people by thinking or feeling for them.

Intimacy flourishes when I allow others the dignity of making their own decisions and accepting their own consequences.

*EXPECTATIONS*

### I REVISE MY UNREALISTIC EXPECTATIONS ABOUT PEOPLE

Today I revise my unrealistic expectations of others. Today I will let go of my fear that trusting others will always bring hurt.

If I have been hurt by others in the past, I know it was not premeditated or intentional. I am realistic enough to know that even if someone loves me, they are only human and not perfect. In my recovery, I grow accepting of human imperfections.

The hurt I might experience as an adult does not have to take on the same devastating significance as it did in the past.

Today I freely choose intimacy with others **despite** past hurts and disappointments. I will examine my expectations and recognize that people are, after all, only human.

*SELF-ACCEPTANCE*

### *ALL THAT I AM IS BEAUTIFUL, AND I CELEBRATE MYSELF TODAY*

Today I am aware of my finest qualities. I am aware of my warmth, my strength, and my beauty.

I need to nurture and care for myself as I would any living thing that I love. Some of us treat our pets far better than we treat ourselves.

Today, I affirm, nurture and reward myself and know that each day I am becoming dearer to myself.

Today I treat myself as I would a dear and loving friend.

*PERFECTION*

## I AM PERFECT, THE BEST THAT I CAN BE, IN THIS MOMENT

Today I'll be the best I can be in this moment. I have sought to be perfect in work, in relationships, and even in leisure. I will not lose sight of the fact that I am human, I'm fallible, I make mistakes and I get over them and move on.

Today I acknowledge my striving for perfection by being all that I can be. I make mistakes and learn from them. Life is not a test where we are constantly being graded for performance.

Today I see that my task is to be the best that I can be. I will experience success and failure at times, and I will learn from each experience.

CHANGE

### *I BELIEVE THAT CHANGE IS POSSIBLE FOR ME*

Today I have the courage to hope and the courage to begin to engage in small changes in my behavior, my feelings and my beliefs. I accept change as a necessary part of living. I embrace change as a necessary part of recovery.

I can see that success is a series of small changes. I envision change as a beautiful pearl. A series of small changes, then, is like an exquisite strand of pearls.

Today I take time to make a plan for change. I chart out areas in my life where changes are needed, and I take steps to put changes in motion. I will not have unrealistic expectations, but I will have patience and perseverance. As I change, I will accept success and failure as part of the process.

*HERE AND NOW*

## I LET GO OF YESTERDAY, AND I FOCUS ON A NEW VISION OF TODAY

I detach myself from yesterday. The beliefs I once had no longer fit my life today. The emotions I once felt served a purpose then, but they interfere with my recovery today. The dreams I dreamt as a child, growing up in an alcoholic home, made life more bearable then, but I dream new dreams now and I have new visions grounded in reality.

I have an ever-expanding awareness of a greater good. I shake free from looking back in anger, fear and guilt. That which has been is now complete, and I release it.

I let go of yesterday and focus on a new vision. Today's dreams are based on balanced expectations. I view today with expanding freedom and joy.

*JOY*

### LAUGHTER AND SMILES
### COME EASY TODAY

I notice that each day I become healthier in recovery. I am able to laugh and express joy. It is a joy to observe what God has made and call it good. With a light heart and joy in my soul, I experience this day.

As the child of an alcoholic, I have learned all I can from misery. I now turn to the creativity of laughter and a deep knowing that life is wonderful. I am aware that what I accept, I become.

This day I accept mentally and emotionally the presence of joy in my life. I speak and think joy in my life.

Today I unselfconsciously laugh with ease, and I smile spontaneously.

*RECOVERY JOURNEY*

## TODAY I REAFFIRM MY COMMITMENT TO RECOVERY

Today I commit myself to my most important project—My Recovery. My recovery, this wonderful broadening of potential, deserves my devotion, my time and my energy.

I give full attention to my recovery journey today. My senses are clear and my self-esteem is enhanced as I honor who I am today. Nothing can sway me from discovering myself. My fear dissolves as I lovingly and honestly look at my present, my past and my Self.

Today I am renewed in this exploration of me called Recovery. And if I find the exploration an arduous one, I know that the struggle will bring a new and gratifying vision of myself.

*RELATIONSHIPS*

## MY HAPPINESS COMES FROM WITHIN, AND I SHARE IT WITH OTHERS

Whenever I enter into a relationship with the idea that another person can make me happy and content, I have begun to fail in that relationship. When I view a relationship in this way, I become concerned over what I might or might not get back.

Today I release my pattern of someone's having to live up to my ideal. I have no right to impose my performance requirements on anyone else.

Today I start relieving others of the responsibility for making me happy. In this way I can begin intimate relationships based upon mutual caring, not on need. This day I acknowledge that I am a full, rich and complete person.

I deserve a relationship, not to make me happy, but to share the richness of who I am in totality with another.

*SEASONS*

## IT'S MY SEASON TO GROW, DEVELOP AND FULFILL MYSELF

Like all living things, I have my own rhythms, my own ebbs and flows, my own seasons of growth and transformation. In recovery, I have phases when, given the right conditions, I can make quantum leaps in my development.

I grow through exploration, and I seek a variety of stimulations. Many of us as toddlers did not have adequate protection to explore and experiment. Because our homes were not child-centered, we had to grow up too fast, too soon. Our need to explore and investigate the world does not go away. Our inability to explore as children lead us, as adults, to symptoms such a lack of motivation, or fatigue, or physical stress reactions.

Today I will take the time to explore my workplace or my home by touch, by sight, by sound, and even by taste. I will give myself the opportunity to continue my development and fill in what I missed in my alcoholic home.

*RESPONSIBILITY*

## I TAKE LOVING RESPONSIBILITY
## FOR MY OWN LIFE

Today I affirm my power to create the kind of existence I choose, and I take loving responsibility for my choices. I do not find others in my past to blame my troubles on.

I realize that life is mine, and I have the power to choose what I want from life—the power to choose what I want to do, and the power to do it well. No one else can control my life but me.

This life is not a rehearsal. I have this chance today to make my life work, to put my energies into recovery and expansion of my potential.

Today I will take time to envision that which I want for myself. I take loving responsibility for my own life.

*LETTING GO*

### TODAY I FEEL AN ASSURANCE OF SERENITY

I stand aside today, and I yield to my Higher Power. I allow the all-harmonizing power of God to resolve and adjust all that concerns me.

The Serenity Prayer asks that we be granted the wisdom to know what we can change and what we cannot. Today I acknowledge those matters that I will release to my Higher Power for resolution. I will not continue to deplete my energies by concentrating on events and circumstances beyond my control.

Today I turn to my Source and feel the harmony that exists when I can let go.

*FEELINGS*

## I ACCEPT ALL MY EMOTIONS
## AND NATURAL EXPRESSIONS

Feelings are part of my nature. Sometimes my feelings are wonderful—sometimes my emotions are painful. Whatever they are, all my feelings are vital and essential in expressing the complete me.

I am a tapestry—an artistic expression of God. The colorful threads that make up this work of art are my emotions. Today I will stand back and view this masterpiece with its many richly blended threads, and I will accept it completely and uncritically.

Today I appreciate that my emotions add color and depth to my life.

*IMAGINATION*

## I CAN BE AN ADULT
## AND STILL BE MAGICAL

Today I will make three wishes for myself. These wishes will be for me, not for anyone else. I will dare to wish for that which I never thought possible for myself.

I have been afraid in the past to think magically. There were too many times in my alcoholic home when dreams did not come true. I gave up wishing, turned my back on prayer, and dreamed no more.

I no longer fear thinking magically, for I have the power to make many of my own wishes come true.

Day by day I am becoming accustomed to thinking about my own desires. As an adult, I can decide what I want for myself.

*INNER SELF*

## TODAY I PULL THE CURTAIN ON MY UNSEEN AUDIENCE

It is not too late to experience joy, to be spontaneous or even outrageous. In order to do this, I must pull the blinds on the critical audience I carry around with me. This audience consists of voices from the past that do not hesitate to tell me when I've messed up, when I'm ridiculous or obnoxious.

Today I resign from doing a performance. I will no longer spend my energies in that way.

Today I will laugh, sing, play and dance—no matter what the voices of my mother or father say. I give myself permission to pull the curtain.

*MY NEEDS*

## I CAN TRUST MYSELF TO KNOW WHAT I NEED

I have complete trust in my ability to determine my own needs. My role is to fully express myself. Today I embrace every opportunity to be who I am. I am not ashamed of my needs.

I am a unique and special individual and my needs are a positive extension of my personhood. There are those who feel they know what is best for me and there are others who tell me what my needs are; I thank them, but I listen to my inner voice. I determine my choices and needs and the directions I'll take in recovery.

Today I am willing to take time to listen to myself. Today I make a conscious decision to trust my inner voice and fulfill my needs.

*SELF-PACING*

## TODAY, I CAN TAKE MY TIME

I'm relaxed today. I'm unrushed, moving at my own pace, getting things accomplished in my own time. I don't have to hurry, I can take my time.

So often in my chemically dependent family, I had to rush to get my needs met. I had to rush to grow up. Today I make a conscious decision to slow down and discover my own timing.

In my own way, I am developing and growing each day. No one can tell me at what rate I should grow.

At this moment, I affirm my own developmental clock that times my growth with exquisite precision. Today, in a relaxed way, I will heed my inner clock. I will respect myself enough to slow down and notice who I am and the beautiful world in which I live.

*LEISURE*

### I CAN ENJOY LEISURE
### WITHOUT GUILT AND ANXIETY

Today I find myself grazing in the pasture called life. Just as a horse doesn't stand at the gate and make a plan before it roams and eats, neither do I feel as if I must constantly have a working plan to relax. It is possible for me to simply watch the grass grow.

I now let go of the belief that all my activities must be goal-oriented. It is not necessary to shame myself for not relaxing in the "right" way.

This day I will give myself the opportunity to experiment with different ways of relaxing. I will give myself permission to decide what things I like to do—even if it means doing nothing!

*HELP*

## I FEEL STRONG ENOUGH TO ASK FOR THE HELP I NEED

I can ask for help in solving my problems. It is important for me to say what I want and how I feel. Making other people guess at my needs simply sets me up to be hurt.

I am capable of handling many projects, but I realize that it's important to ask for help if I need it.

I am a powerful person. I also acknowledge that I am not a Superperson. As I mature, I have the strength to ask for help before my problems become overpowering. I don't have to do it alone.

*SELF-RESPECT*

## I RESPECT MYSELF AND OTHERS

Day by day, I am having more respect for myself and for other people.

Gradually I am freeing myself from feeling obliged to perform. I don't have to be cute or do tricks to get my needs met. My rewards come not only from what I do, but from who I am.

Everyone has needs, and today I am opening myself up to acknowledge my own. In doing so, I allow other people the dignity of acknowledging theirs.

*MENTAL HEALTH*

### I CONSCIOUSLY CHOOSE HEALTHY THOUGHTS AND BALANCED EMOTIONS

I refuse to be depressed by negative beliefs that might have come from my family of origin. I refuse to constrict my thinking by concentrating on beliefs that limit my experience.

Today I acknowledge that I have emotions—but I am not my emotions. This means that my emotions and thoughts can flow through my consciousness, but I need not be swept away by the tide. Today I am selecting those beliefs that are healthy for me.

I take a few moments to quiet my thoughts today. I find a quiet place and concentrate on my breathing. I select only healthy thoughts and emotions and let the rest drift away.

Today I greet my feelings like old and dear friends who want to visit for a bit and then leave again.

*PATIENCE*

## I TAKE GREAT PATIENCE
## WITH MY RECOVERY

It's all right to feel whatever I'm feeling now. I don't have to feel perfect every day.

Oftentimes in my recovery, I've wondered why I don't feel good immediately. If I'm working on my issues, it seems like everything should just fall in place.

I understand there's no cure or fix for being human, and changing emotions is part of the process of normal living.

Today I possess the patience and the wisdom to start from where I am and move forward. I appreciate myself and my emotions.

*ANGER*

### *I CAN EXPRESS MY ANGER OPENLY, HONESTLY AND APPROPRIATELY*

I am not afraid of my anger. Learning to get angry is an important developmental key to being able to separate from my family. In my alcoholic home, anger was not tolerated and I was shamed for exhibiting healthy emotions.

Today, I know that my anger is one way to create boundaries for myself. At this moment, I accept my anger as an important vehicle of expression. I can make decisions to express my anger honestly, openly and appropriately.

Sometimes when I hang on to anger, it boils and turns into rage. It is then that I become afraid to express myself.

I have the right to express anger when I feel it.

## I WILL TAKE CARE OF
## MY PERSONAL NEEDS

Today I will attend to my needs; I will make my day a day of healing amd I will attend to my physical, spiritual and emotional needs. So often in my alcoholic family my needs were discounted and ignored. I resolve to take care of myself now.

Today I will eat well-balanced meals, and get the rest necessary to replenish my body.

Today I will express my feelings freely with the reassuring help of others. I will surround myself with people whom I trust to give me the support I need.

Today I acknowledge that I am important to God. I will take a few moments during the day to allow the love of God to enfold me.

*SELF-KNOWLEDGE*

## I OBSERVE MYSELF WITH
## COMPASSION AND LOVE

I am learning day by day to observe myself compassionately instead of abusively. The task is to KNOW MYSELF. In order to gain self-knowledge, I must observe myself in my interactions with others.

Today I will focus on what needs and desires I have. In my alcoholic family, so much of my energy was "other-directed," I was concerned with others more than I was concerned with myself. Consequently, I never developed a sense of my own identity.

From this moment, I will embark on a search for myself. For this search, I will equip myself with complete love and compassion.

*FEELINGS*

## I CAN EXPRESS MY FEELINGS
## IN A DIRECT WAY

I will not harm people by telling them what I feel. By communicating feelings directly, I am respecting myself by owning my own power.

In my alcoholic family, I learned to communicate my feelings indirectly. Feelings were forbidden and hidden—they had to be guessed at, and deduced from clues in behavior.

This indirect style no longer works for me. I don't want to play games with people where my feelings are concerned. I don't want to leave a trail of clues for others to use in solving the mystery of my emotional life.

Today I will communicate in a healthy and direct manner. I make a conscious decision to make my feelings known in a direct and appropriate way.

*HEALTH*

## I VISUALIZE MYSELF
## IN GOOD PHYSICAL HEALTH

Today I cleanse my body of all impurities. My body is a gift that deserves my best attention. Today I will nurture my body with healthy **food**, healthy **acceptance**, and healthy **thoughts.**

I am happy with who I am, and I enthusiastically accept and enjoy my physical identity. I breathe deeply, concentrating on thoughts of wellness as I inhale. And as I exhale, all negativity and impurities flow from me.

My body receives the impression of my every thought, therefore, I will always give it powerful suggestions of health.

Today I revel in my good health.

*CHILDHOOD*

### TODAY I REVIEW MY CHILDHOOD WITHOUT SHAME

I review my childhood with a new perspective. I realize that the chaos and inconsistencies in my alcoholic family were not my fault. Although I felt blamed and criticized for being the cause of my parents' chemical dependency, I know I was not at fault.

I was the best child I could be. My family's sickness was **not** because I was bad, not good enough, or imperfect. The disease of alcoholism prevented my parents from expressing love in a healthy way. I am not responsible for what happened in my family.

As I move through recovery, I will not blame myself today for what has taken place yesterday. I am not ignoring my past; rather, I am choosing to understand the past and the effect it has on my adult life.

Today I can examine my childhood memories without shame or guilt. I was not responsible for the chaos and inconsistency in my home.

*DANGEROUS FEELINGS*

### I LISTEN TO MY FEELINGS AND LET GO OF YESTERDAY'S PAIN

Today I begin to make peace with my personal history. Unresolved childhood trauma will cease to contaminate my adult life. One of the important steps I can take in letting go of a piece of personal history is to work through my feelings.

My feelings tell me exactly what has happened and what I need to do. I can turn my full attention to my feelings and think about ways to resolve them. I am confident that my feelings will not overpower me, drive me insane, or kill those around me. Feelings that were dangerous for me to express in my family when I was growing up have no such power today.

Today I will look at the feelings I have about myself. Many negative feelings are childhood leftovers and have no basis in my current reality. As I face the memories that haunt me, I will start to let go of yesterday's pain.

*HAPPINESS*

### MY HAPPINESS DEPENDS ON ME

Today I react positively to my environment, and to the people around me. I look at life with a new understanding of what is important. My happiness depends on ME—and only I can make a hell or a heaven on earth for myself. My happiness does not depend on other people or outer circumstances.

My happiness does not depend upon another's feelings toward me—it depends on how well I like myself. My happiness does not depend upon my income, on where I live or what I own. My happiness depends upon how clearly I can see the spiritual reality behind all appearances.

I take responsibility for my happiness today, and I let cheerfulness and good will pervade all that I do.

*UNFINISHED BUSINESS*

## TODAY I WILL ATTEND TO LOOSE ENDS

Today I declare myself motivated. I possess all the strength and stamina I need to succeed in my recovery. In the past, I have looked to other people for my motivation. Today is the day I take my life into my own hands. I have all the abilities I need to accomplish any task.

Today I turn to my Higher Source to provide me with the inspiration I need to break negative habits of thinking and behaving.

I give my attention this day to unfinished business. I am able to complete what is before me with enthusiasm. I have the power to make this a day of accomplishment.

*FREEDOM*

## I DECLARE MYSELF FREE
## TO GO FORWARD

Today I am free to go forward. I am free from the constraints of the past. I visualize any destructive thoughts or addictive behavior as washed away. I release all that has gone before, and I am free to have the kind of life I long for.

I am not bound to old and limited ways of thinking. I see beyond old patterns of personal consciousness that have imprisoned me.

I am not bound to old habits or traits that I want to overcome. I free myself from the constraints of old behavior patterns. People and things do not have control over my spirit.

I am in charge of my mind, my body, and my affairs. My spirit is free, and I give thanks.

*CHANGE FOR THE BETTER*

## RIGHT NOW MY LIFE IS CHANGING FOR THE BETTER

New and inviting ways are opening for me each day. I have no limitations, for I am mightier than circumstances.

I don't have to depend upon others for my fulfillment, for I have the will, the vitality and strength to push away the old patterns that bind me.

The world is mine to become whatever I want within it. My hopes and dreams are all within reach. I do not fret about my future, because I have the power to change. I will choose what I want to happen and let it unfold with trust and love.

Today I know that I am in control, and that I can confidently change my life in order to find fulfillment.

*INNER CHILD*

## I OPEN MY HEART
## TO MY INNER CHILD

The child within me is playful, beautiful and expressive. There is a child within me that needs love and attention. My child self is an important part of who I am. In my alcoholic home, I never had time to be a child. It is this precious child that knows how to play and accept love. It is this precious child that I am discovering.

Throughout the day I will let the memories of my childhood flow. Whether they are painful or pleasant, I know that these memories will help me discover an important part of myself that I have ignored. I feel a natural affinity with my child self, and I know that I can love and accept it. I will nurture the child within me with tenderness and warmth. As I love and accept the child within me, I feel the wonderfully playful part of me emerge.

Today I open my heart to my child self, knowing that it still lives within me.

*HAPPINESS NOW*
## I AM HAPPY NOW

I am happy NOW. I do not have to wait for my alcoholic parent to recover. I do not have to defer my own happiness to accommodate someone else's schedule. I can be happy now.

I have a right to pursue a productive, fulfilling life. I have a right to pursue a life of health and sanity without feeling guilty because others remain stuck. I can make changes and live the way I want to. My happiness is not dependent upon my parents' sobriety, recovery or acknowledgment of their problem.

I can detach. I can refuse to participate in destructive behavior. I can resist the temptation to be the "fixer" or the "victim" or the "super-hero." I trust my feelings to help me know when to detach.

Today I decide to be happy. Today I decide that my parents' problems belong to them and not to me. I feel free and enthusiastic and I bless myself, my family, and this day.

*FREEDOM*

## TODAY I AFFIRM MY FREEDOM FROM ADDICTION OF ANY KIND

I am alive and free!

So often I have followed a spiritual calling by going to the wrong address. What I strive for is wholeness—completeness and integration. I know now that serenity will not be found in chemicals, relationships, or in any unhealthy dependency.

In my search for meaning, I might have turned to chemicals, food, and relationships—only to emerge feeling empty, numb and confused. Today I stop depending upon people and things for my fulfillment. Today I declare myself free from unhealthy dependencies. I am a child of God and I am learning to see myself as God sees me.

My consciousness is awakened by the news that I have what it takes to live a full and productive life. Today I affirm my life and my freedom from addiction of any kind.

*BALANCE*

### *I AM LEARNING A SENSE OF BALANCE*

I am learning a sense of balance—I don't have to live with extremes. The world is not black and white, but full of beautiful hues and rich shades of color. So, too, my experiences and emotions are rich and in balance. I am learning to see the world.

Today I don't have to be "right" or "wrong." I can experience myself in perfect balance: In my intake of food, I neither abstain nor do I gorge; in my relationships, I am neither fused nor am I isolated; in my friendships, I am neither trusting to an unrealistic degree, nor am I distrustful of everyone.

One of the important gifts I can give myself is learning my own sense of balance. Today, I choose to let go of old patterns that are destructive. I am no longer living with an alcoholic parent, and I choose to release all extreme behaviors, beliefs, and emotions that keep me off balance.

*INDIVIDUALITY*

## I DARE TO BE MYSELF

The power of God lives in all that I do and all that I am. It is my gift to express God's presence through my life. The choice is mine—whether to hide my uniqueness, or to freely dance to the special music that I hear.

When I strive to be who I am **supposed** to be, rather than who I **am**, I pay the price. The price is very high: Physical illness, unhappiness, restlessness, or addiction. Today, I choose the road to health, sanity and serenity.

I will express myself in ways that I never have before. Today I will dare to be myself.

*INNER VOICE*

## I WILL GIVE MYSELF
## POSITIVE MESSAGES

I will befriend myself by ceasing to create my own anxieties. What are those inner voices that constantly stir up pain and fear? Those are left-over, critical voices from my past that told me I was a bad, worthless person. Perhaps the last hold-out to my recovery is facing my shame.

Shame is like a hidden monster in the closet that pops out when I don't expect it. The messages that hit right at my core originate in my shamefulness. The journey through shame requires me to turn these inner thoughts outward. I recognize shame when I feel it and substitute these negative voices with positive affirmations.

Today, I begin a new phase of my recovery as I realize that some of the anxiety I feel is self-induced shame. I have the courage to treat myself with kindness and let old wounds heal.

*RULES*

## I CAN CHANGE THE RULES

Today I see that I can safely examine the rules I live by and that I have the power to change them if I want, to promote my recovery.

Am I still living unconsciously by rules that no longer fit me? In my alcoholic family, there were many rules that were incongruent and unrealistic.

Today I will look at my rules about love, money, friends, sex, decisions, and emotions. Which rules are my choices, which rules have I unconsciously adopted?

I have the ability to decide which rules work for me and discard those that do not.

\* \* \* \* \* \*

Suggestion: List the categories mentioned above. Write down the rules in each category from your family of origin. Now write down **your** rules. Are they the same? Have you unconsciously accepted them?

*BURNOUT*

## I CAN HELP OTHER PEOPLE AND STILL TAKE CARE OF MY OWN NEEDS

I will take care of myself and prevent getting "burned out." I can take care of my own needs, and I can help other people. If I fail to care for myself and become exhausted, lethargic and angry, I will be able to help no one at all.

I run the risk of getting burned out when I give wholly to others that which I need myself. I do others an injustice when I don't take care of myself, but I do myself the gravest injustice of all.

I will find the nourishment and support I need from those I trust. I will take time to relax and unwind. When I see to it that my own needs are met, I am not tempted to fill my unmet needs in ways that harm myself and others. Today I resolve to attend to my needs before I attempt to help someone else. I will find nurturing and support from my friends and my Higher Power. And in seeing to it that I get my own needs met, I will prevent burnout. I will not be tempted to fill my unmet needs in ways that will harm me.

ACCOMPLISHMENT

## I AM ABLE TO FINISH PROJECTS THAT I BEGIN

Today I will look at my tasks with new eyes. I will not overgeneralize my projects and become overwhelmed with the big picture. Neither will I become bogged down with detail.

I enter new projects with a consciousness of balance and persistence. If I need help, I will ask for it, and I will not be ashamed to seek assistance. I am not expected to know everything. I am not expected to achieve perfection in all situations. Instead, I can do my best in all that I undertake.

Today I can set up a plan of action towards accomplishment and know that I can succeed one step at a time.

*SELF-SACRIFICE*

### I CAN GET WHAT I NEED
### WITHOUT SUFFERING

I can get taken care of just because I am who I am—a valuable human being. I don't have to get headaches or ulcers, and I don't need to drop from nervous exhaustion so that others will pay attention and care for me.

In my family, sometimes the only way I got attention was to get sick. Even though this isn't true today, I might ignore my needs until I become physically ill.

Today I will take the time to listen to my body. If I am tired, tense, or need to be touched, I will attend to any needs that I have.

I will remember that the old rules from my alcoholic family **no longer apply**. I will not sacrifice myself to get attention and approval.

*RELAXING*

### *I WILL BREATHE, I WILL FEEL, I WILL RELAX*

Today I will commit myself to three basic tasks that mark a new beginning: I will breathe, I will feel, I will relax.

Today I will take a moment for retreat. When I don't give myself the solitude I need, I have no chance to replenish myself.

Today I will remember how to breathe. With all that is happening in my life, I sometimes get blocked and take short, shallow gasps of air. I almost forget how important it is to breathe deeply and let fresh air fill my lungs. I nourish myself when I take deep and long breaths.

Today I will allow myself to feel. By experiencing all of my emotions, I can respond more fully to the richness life has to offer.

Today I will remember to breathe, I allow myself to feel and to take time for solitude. These are basic spiritual, physical and emotional ingredients that allow me to flourish.

HARMONY

## I AM BALANCED AND CENTERED IN ALL THAT I DO TODAY

Today I will take a moment to become balanced and find my center. When I am centered, nothing can disturb or upset me. Centered, I am peaceful, agreeable and in harmony.

In the past, my alcoholic home was out of balance. Discord and turmoil prevailed over harmony and peace. In my alcoholic home, my childhood models schooled me in emotional extremes, inconsistency and distrust. Today I let the past rest and I seek a balanced and congruent existence.

Today I will experiment with different ways of becoming centered and at peace. I choose to discover that quiet place within. I keep myself centered in the harmony of God's love and release self-defeating thoughts from my mind.

*ADULTHOOD*

### I CELEBRATE MY
### ADULTHOOD TODAY

I'm glad that I'm growing up. As I move through recovery, I can begin to take satisfaction in adulthood. Part of becoming my own friend means reclaiming my adult self so that it becomes an active, yet flexible voice in my inner dialogue. This voice helps me to behave responsibly with myself and with others.

I will use my adult self to check with reality to make sure my expectations are congruent. I will use my adult self to make choices that are in my best interests, and to think ahead to logical consequences.

In my alcoholic home, growing up was never celebrated. I concluded that becoming an adult meant losing the love and support of those around me. My behavior would reflect this by remaining childish, dependent and resistant to growth.

Today I affirm that I am lovable at all ages. I will celebrate my adulthood and use my mature wisdom to guide me.

*PHYSICAL HEALTH*

## MY PHYSICAL WELL-BEING IS IMPORTANT TO ME

Part of nurturing myself means taking good care of my body. I will not deny reality by believing that I can disregard my health and still feel vital and strong. Growing up with critical parents taught me to be overly demanding of myself and to be unaware of my own needs.

If I load my body with inappropriate food, if I refuse myself adequate rest, or if I bulldoze through one stressful situation after another, I am abusing myself.

How do I begin to take care of my body? I can begin by **not** demanding more than my body can physically handle. I can learn to say "No!" to activities that deplete my energy. Finally, I can eat well and get adequate sleep and exercise.

I will not expect to change all my habits overnight. Gentleness, not perfection, is the key word today. With a consciousness of health, I pursue healthy living.

INVENTORY

## TODAY I WILL FACE MY UNCOMFORTABLE EMOTIONS AND I WILL BEGIN TO WORK THROUGH THEM

I will face my emotions today and let them pass. How do I deal with uncomfortable feelings? Have I adopted strategies that are healthy for me, or am I repeating the self-destructive patterns of my alcoholic family? As I become conscious of my behavior, I might see my childhood lived out in my adulthood.

When I am feeling unconfident or insecure, do I run to the security of relationships, shopping, or excessive physical release to feel better? If I have a tendency to overspend, overeat, or just plain over-do when I am upset, I want to change the pattern. When I over-do anything, it never feels right. During these times of excess, I feel as though I am trying to fill up a bottomless pit. If I continue to run from my emotions, I will continue to suffer the consequences. Today I will face my uncomfortable feelings and begin to work through them.

*CRITICISM*

# I CAN HANDLE CRITICISM WITH EASE

I em entitled to my own thoughts, and others are entitled to theirs. When people form opinions of my behavior, I feel calm and at ease. I can choose how I view the opinions and judgments of others. I will not use the opinions of others as ammunition against myself.

In the past, I let criticism from others trigger my shame. The negative reactions of others seemed to prove how bad I really was.

No more. I will not let the response of others control my behavior or my feelings. Today I will simply notice, without anxiety or shame, that others have opinions. If I choose to change my behavior, it will be to please myself—not anyone else.

*EXPECTATIONS*

### *I HAVE THE COURAGE TO VIEW LIFE WITH REALISTIC EXPECTATIONS*

I can view situations with realism when I am grounded in truth. A sure way to create misery for myself is to broaden the gap between my hope and my reality. When I live by impossible expectations and distorted myths about people, I am often disappointed.

What are some of the expectations that I live with? Do I expect others to always understand my feelings? Do I expect that now that I am in a relationship I will never feel lonely and unloved?

In my alcoholic family, I was constantly disappointed. Do I still punish myself by holding on to rigid ideas about myself or others? As an adult, refusing to alter my expectations is a set-up for failure.

Viewing life with realism means living by the Serenity Prayer. I possess the wisdom to know the difference between that which I need to accept and that which I can change.

*SHAME /SELF-TALK*

## TODAY I DISCARD BELIEFS
## THAT HINDER MY RECOVERY

Today I am aware of my thoughts and I realize that my world is a reflection of all that I believe. I acknowledge that my beliefs manifest themselves in my reality; therefore, I have no time for negative thinking, no time for destructive thoughts or beliefs that hinder my recovery.

I discard the emotions of guilt, shame and resentment. I am not guilty, and I have no reason to feel shame. I let my resentments flow away as I experience the comfort and security of my Higher Power.

Today I release those beliefs that are destructive, that have outlived their usefulness. Today my thoughts center on beauty, abundance, order, love, freedom, and health.

*SELF-RESPONSIBILITY*

## I AM RESPONSIBLE FOR MYSELF

I am responsible **to** the people I work with. I am not responsible **for** them. Feeling responsible for others results in over-controlling, manipulative behavior. Always being in control means that if my clients don't succeed in therapy, it's my fault. It means that if my students don't learn what I'm teaching them, then surely I am the one to blame.

Being responsible for others is part of the shaming, addictive alcoholic system. What this system taught me is that if something doesn't go my way, I must use what-ever works to achieve my goal. This might mean blaming others, behaving seductively, being weak, sick, or even changing the subject. I delude myself into believing that I can control the outcome of any situation.

Today I realize that I do not control life. I do not know how things are supposed to go, or how others are to achieve their lives' purposes. Responsibility to others means simply that I will do the best job I can do. I will respect the dignity of others to realize their own responsibility.

*POWER*

## I CAN BE POWERFUL AND
## STILL BE AT PEACE

The presence of my Higher Power exists in me. I do not have to reach outside myself for what dwells within. I am involved in a search for peace of mind. I desire to feel good about myself emotionally, physically, mentally and spiritually. Achieving this state of happiness will not come by focusing on material things or on other people.

I feel peaceful when I recognize the tremendous power that exists within me. When I align myself with my inner power, I know that I align myself with God. I have seen what happens when my power isn't put to good use. This is when I begin to depend on people and things to fill me up.

I am no longer weighed down by people and things. Through my recovery, I am discovering ways to align myself with my inner power and with God, so that I can move forward in fulfilling my potential.

*GENTLENESS*

## I AM GENTLE WITH MYSELF
## AND RESPECTFUL OF OTHERS

Today I will be gentle with myself and show tenderness for others. I will experience this day without demanding perfection from myself or others. When I become harsh toward myself, this harshness spills over into my relationships. When I am critical and demanding, I pave the way for loneliness and I limit my own development.

To promote my recovery, I live each moment treating myself with gentleness and kindness.

Today, I can admit that I have weaknesses without becoming shameful or overwhelmed. I will not run away from myself for being human, nor will I destroy my relationships by being overly critical and demanding. These leftovers from my alcoholic home can be cast away forever.

I feel renewed and encouraged as I concentrate less on finding the correct answers to my problems and more on how I am treating myself along the way. As I learn to take care of myself, answers will come.

*SEXUALITY*

## I ACCEPT AND AFFIRM
## MY SEXUALITY TODAY

I'm glad I am a woman. I'm glad I am a man.

Our culture has sent us mixed messages about what it means to be a boy (man) or a girl (woman). Many of us have grown up with distorted views about our sex roles.

It is important to develop our own versions of what it means to be male or female. While we are involved in this self discovery, it is also important to get extra assurance from those close to us.

Affirming our masculinity or femininity has nothing to do with sexism. As men and women, we recognize that we possess both male and female characteristics. As we achieve wholeness, we discover and appreciate the beauty of both these qualities.

Today we affirm our sex and acknowledge that it is wonderful to be a man or a woman.

*CHOICE*

### I WILL THINK BEFORE
### I ACT TODAY

I have the wisdom to know that I must think before I act, today and every day. In my alcoholic home, decisions were made impulsively. The results were inconsistency, chaos and unpredictability, all of which made it risky to count on anything for sure.

I must make choices in my recovery and I must act on them, but I must think before I act. This is not indecisiveness, but rather a disciplined decision to avoid impulsiveness in my behavior.

If I have been floundering about, trying to satisfy my desires without success, perhaps I need to take the time to listen to my inner voice. If I have been bound by outer things, by what people think, say or do, perhaps I need to pause and decide what I really want.

I will take my thoughts seriously today. I will live creatively and effectively as I continue to think before I act.

*PLEASURE*

## I GIVE MYSELF PERMISSION TO ENJOY LIFE

I am giving myself permission to enjoy life. For much of my life, pleasure was an award that I had to earn. I was taught to set aside my own desires in favor of pleasing others. I was taught that to have fun was a waste of time, and if I were experiencing pleasure, I couldn't be doing the "right thing."

Today I challenge and re-assess all that I have been taught about pleasure. Pleasure is not a reward for something I do. It is the most essential experience of my living. My physical and spiritual self is organized to move toward pleasure and away from pain. A sure indicator that I am growing in the right direction is that I can experience joy and pleasure. I desire joy in my activities today as I give myself permission to appreciate my own magnificence. I can learn that my greatest pleasure comes not from **doing**, but from **being**.

Through my recovery, I realize that struggle and tension are not necessarily sure signs that I am doing my best. The real indicator of high functioning and wholeness is experiencing joy.

*SELF-APPROVAL*

## *I CAN HONOR MYSELF WITHOUT SEARCHING FOR APPROVAL*

Today I no longer feel the desperate need to have everyone's approval. I will not submerge my real self to gain the approval of all. As an adult, I do not need to blindly seek the "OK" stamp from everyone, for everything.

I grew up with a "criticizer" in my consciousness that demanded perfection. I grew up trying to please everyone to obtain love. I reject that script today. I challenge the old belief that I'll be rejected for being me.

Today I will relate to others with an inner conviction that I have worth. If this isn't natural for me, I will act as if it is. I will imagine myself as someone who feels self-worth and inner integrity. I will notice what it feels like and how I behave.

I will not go through life apologizing. I will not go through life being a self-defeating pleaser. Now that I am learning to love myself, I do not need to please everyone.

Today, I approve of myself.

*SELF-WORTH*
## TODAY I ACCEPT MY MISTAKES

I embrace my lack of perfection, and I accept my mistakes. I have the right to be wrong. My self-worth does not have to evaporate when I fall short of my expectations. Giving myself permission to be human means that I can withhold self-judgment. I will not dwell on past mistakes. Yesterday ended at midnight, and I recognize that there is a statute of limitations on past errors. I do not have to pay and pay forever. Unless I forgive myself, I will not be able to operate in the present with self-esteem.

Today I welcome my lack of perfection. My mistakes have taught me things that I'll never forget. It is through my mistakes that I become aware of areas in which I need to grow. Whatever I did in the past was the best I could do under the particular limitations at that time. To treat myself with a firm gentleness means that I can face my mistakes calmly and take appropriate action without feeling ashamed.

ACCOMPLISHMENT

### TODAY I GIVE MYSELF
### PERMISSION TO SUCCEED

Today I give myself full permission to succeed. I will turn down the volume on all negative messages that tell me otherwise. I will avoid the incongruent paterns of my family of origin. I will not pay lip service about believing in myself, while complaining about all the obstacles that keep me stuck.

I do not have to have exceptional ability, a genius I.Q., or perfect conditions in order to be successful. Using my God-given abilities, I will create my own conditions that will allow me to blossom.

I have the determination and confidence to function at my full potential. I will no longer sabotage my success by setting unattainable goals, overscheduling myself, or working myself into a frenzy. I will not work so hard that I undermine my ability to be inspired.

Today I remind myself that a sign of success is the ability to laugh and enjoy the pleasure of daily living.

*WHOLENESS*

## I CAN SEPARATE MYSELF
## FROM MY WORK

I want to enjoy my work and feel that I am making a contribution. I do not want to become addicted to my job and use work as a means of protecting myself from my feelings. It is important to me to be able to derive enjoyment from non-working activities. I need to be able to separate myself from my job so that I can develop and maintain relationships with family and friends.

If I am only truly happy when I am working, I may be neglecting other parts of myself that need enrichment. If I am content only when I am pressured by responsibility, I may be in flight from fears of inadequacy or failure.

In all parts of my life, I am searching for balance. If I am defined only by what I do at work, I need to take an inventory of my emotional, physical, and spiritual life. Changing my work habits may require compromises and a new philosophy of life. (I will not allow the alcoholic pattern of denial prevent me from taking control of my life.) I am creating a future of inner joy and balance.

*FLEXIBILITY*

## MY LIFE EXPRESSES A SPIRIT
## OF FLEXIBILITY

I am learning to be flexible in my approach to life. Day by day, I am adjusting my attitudes and my rigid schedule to accommodate the unexpected. I am open to new beliefs and new ways of doing things. I release the rigid codes of behavior that others are expected to live up to.

Life is filled with all kinds of interesting people and a great variety of experiences. An infinite amount of potential and possibilities exist for me if I am open to them. As I learn to trust myself, I am able to be flexible, adaptable, and less resistant to change.

Today I release outmoded habits of thinking and feeling. My life possesses a balance of structure and spontaneity that allows me to experience new ideas and new situations. My life expresses a spirit of flexibility, and with this comes peace, contentment and well-being.

*HIGHER POWER*

### GOD IS ALWAYS WITH ME

As I go about my activities today, I will be aware of God's presence within me. If I have errands to run or work to do, or if I am involved in duties at home, I will keep an awareness of God's presence in my mind and my heart. I am never separated from the protecting presence of the Higher Source. This all-encompassing Presence is with me at all times and in all places.

There may have been times in my past when I thought that God had deserted me. Perhaps my search for meaning had left me discouraged and disappointed.

Today I realize that my Higher Power dwells inside of me. If I am in need of reassurance or protection, I will remember that I can never be where God is not. Whatever my needs are, large or small, I can turn to my Eternal Source for help.

Today I envision myself supported and enfolded in the hands of God. I let go of fear and anxiety as I feel the protective presence of my Higher Power.

*SELF-DECEPTION*
## I AM FREE FROM THE PRISON OF DELUSION

I will no longer deceive myself. I will no longer stifle my impulse toward growth. By refusing to change, I avoid any confrontation with my dreams or hopes. Keeping myself stuck lets me avoid the risk of failure and is fertile ground for denial.

As a child, I developed a high tolerance for inappropriate situations. It was safer to delude myself than suffer the possible consequences of rejection. The consequences of self-deceit are depression and a nagging dissatisfaction. In order to avoid my feelings at any cost, I talk myself into a peaceful delusion. I would rather believe that my life must remain flat than risk making an adventure out of the future.

Today I can venture into unknown emotional territory. I can examine my relationships, my job, my family, and make decisions based on today, The choice to remain the way I am is always a choice—but, at least, it is a conscious one.

*SELF-ACCEPTANCE*

## AS I GROW IN SELF-ACCEPTANCE I BECOME A RADIATING CENTER OF ENCOURAGEMENT

Today I will provide encouragement to myself and to others around me. Criticism, rejection and fear have discouraged me in the past. When I get discouraged, I act out, become defensive and get locked in a private belief system that justifies everything I do perfectly. Discouragement is a relic from the past that I now bury and put to rest.

I remind myself that criticism is one of the most potent instruments of discouragement. Criticism is one of the chief methods of undermining self-esteem. This means that as a parent, I am not helping my children when I ridicule them. I am not helping anyone overcome self-consciousness by shaming them.

Today, I will practice self-acceptance and acceptance of others, despite their shortcomings. This doesn't mean that I have to tolerate unacceptable behavior, but rather that I try to provide encouragement to others whenever possible.

*ACCOMPLISHMENT*

### *I ACKNOWLEDGE MY ABILITIES AND THE ABILITIES OF OTHERS*

I deserve to be given credit for my accomplishments. So do others. When I discount the accomplishments or work of others, it usually means one of two things—a false confidence in myself, or the need to inflate my own ego. I don't need to make myself feel better by maliciously putting others down.

Acknowledging the ability of others is something I never learned as a child. In my family, one had to be always **Number One** to get recognition.

Today I know I don't have to be perfect to get credit and appreciation from others. I will give others credit for their skills, their contributions, their accomplishments—regardless of their status or position in life.

I will remember that it takes mutual respect for an organization or a family to work. It takes different temperaments, talents, and abilities for a group to be successful. Today I will honor my abilities and the abilities of others.

*THE PAST*

## YESTERDAY IS FINISHED— I AM READY FOR TODAY

I unclutter my consciousness today, and rid myself of old patterns, old hurts and wrong beliefs. I close the book on yesterday and focus my thoughts on today. Equipped with fresh ideas, feelings and new ways of living, I am now free to proceed with the business of life. I already have everything I need to do this.

I am changing into a more effective person. With joy, I banish fear and guilt from my mind. I let go of the outworn ideas, the futile emotions, the anguish and uncertainty that have been obstacles to my recovery. Yesterday is finished—I am ready to get on with the business of today.

My recovery is not dependent upon the resolution of yesterday's problems. Those problems are relevant only as they apply to today. My recovery takes place in the present.

Each day is God's gift to me. I respect the good, the beauty, and even the pain I have known. However, I keep my thinking and feeling centered on this day.

*CURIOSITY AND CREATIVITY*

### I CELEBRATE ALL OF MY SENSES TODAY

Thoreau once said, "Only that day dawns to which we are awake." Each day comes and goes. The beauty of life is lost when I wander through moments unconsciously. I will delight in fully experiencing this day by wakening my senses.

To do this, I need to give my inner child permission to come out of hiding. What gave me pleasure as a small child? Sniffing oranges as I peeled the skin? Rolling a caramel around in my mouth? Feeling the swooping thrill as I swished down a slide? Playing with bubbles in a soapy bath?

What a great loss it is when I fail to enjoy all my senses. I will remember that my ability to recapture is there for the taking. The curiosity and creativity I possessed as a child is still inside of me.

Today I will allow myself to pursue activities which will awaken my senses. Whether dancing, writing, playing, or listening, I celebrate the creative wonderful parts that I possess.

### NATURAL ORDER

## I WILL LOOK OUTSIDE MYSELF AND NOTICE THE BEAUTY AROUND ME

All is in order. There is nothing I have to do at this moment to alter the universe. As I behold this lush green day, there is a sense of oneness with all living things.

No matter what I do or do not do, the clouds will still roll by, the sun will still shine, the stars will stay on course. When life seems chaotic and disordered, I can look to nature and feel secure in the presence of a Higher Order.

Just as the seasons follow one after another, so do I have my own growing seasons. This summer is a time to realize my potential and absorb all that life has to offer. The fragrant air, the singing birds, the feel of the warm wind against my face—all this is mine, and more.

This summer's day, I allow myself to grow and blossom. This season I will pull in nourishment from all my sources and thoroughly revel in all that is mine to enjoy.

*EXCELLENCE*

## *TODAY I WILL THINK THE VERY BEST AND DRAW THE VERY BEST TO MYSELF*

As I believe, so I am. I have heard these words many times. Now I will put them into action and see them become facts in my life. No longer do I waste time condemning myself for my inadequacies or blaming the past for my failures. I am ready to allow the positive to express itself in my life. This is something only I can do. No one else can do it for me.

My recovery is a process of uncovering the real beauty that is deep inside of me. I have faith that this beauty is there, and it is with genuine determination that my search is successful. Only my own negativity can keep my beautiful light from shining out deep within me. I can move forward in the light or live in darkness. Knowing that light promotes life and growth, I come into the light.

Today I will expect the very best, and therefore I will see the very best. God is with me, leading and directing me toward the light of recovery.

*NEW DAY*

## A NEW DAY HAS BEEN GIVEN TO ME TO EXPERIENCE THAT WHICH I DESIRE

How did I wake up this morning? With a heavy feeling wondering how I was ever going to get through today? Or did I wake up relaxed, ready for anything, and expecting only the best to come to me? If I awakened full of stress and tension, it's time to change my attitude **now**. Not another moment will go by with my thoughts still attuned to yesterday's problems and dilemmas. I have no desire to drag the old behind me into this new day.

I see that I can make or ruin the day by the way I approach it. At this moment, I wake up to the fact that I have free choice, and I will exercise it consciously. I will use this day carefully, knowing that time is precious. Enough time has been wasted in self blame, rigidity, and remorse.

If I have problems that need solving, I will keep myself open to all possibilities. With this attitude, I will find the help I need, possibly right before my eyes. I have much to learn today, and I am ready for wonderful things to unfold.

*INDEPENDENCE*

## I DECLARE MY EMOTIONAL INDEPENDENCE FROM MY PARENTS

I am coming to terms with the values and expectations that were imposed by my parents. The process of declaring my independence from my family continues on into adulthood. Today I give myself permission to emotionally separate from my family of origin.

Choosing different values and beliefs from those of my parents may cause me to feel guilty. I might need to reassure myself that I am not "letting my family down" by becoming an adult.

Deciding upon my own path is the most important task I must accomplish. If I allow guilt to stand in my way, I will have to face a life filled with resentment, suffocation and a diminished sense of my own worth.

I declare my emotional independence from my parents today, with love and respect for them and for myself. I have the courage and wisdom to discern which values and beliefs are useful to me and which I will no longer live by.

*HEALING POWER*

### AS A HELPER, I RECOGNIZE THE HEALING POWER IN ALL

Every so often, the enormity and complexity of my work give me the impression that there is little I can really do to help other people. I may become frustrated and overwhelmed with the problems of others. And with this powerlessness, I may become controlling.

As a helper, I must not lose sight of the fact that I am not a guru—I am a catalyst. It is not my job to provide others with "The Answers." Rather, I can be a powerful change agent, providing others with opportunities to discover their own solutions.

When I impose my beliefs on my clients, I inhibit the growth process. I can and will allow others the dignity of self-discovery. If others disagree or choose alternatives that I don't agree with, I will not become enraged at their disobedience.

I believe in the inherent beauty and strength in all human beings, and I will not assume that I know what's best for everyone. Instead, I will model decisiveness, strength, security, and inner peace that will reverberate to those around me.

(186)

---

*BALANCE*

### I PUT MY ENERGY TO GOOD USE

I am learning to channel my energies in a purposeful direction. I have something special to contribute to this world, and I am in the process of learning what this "specialness" is all about. I will not waste my energies by flitting from one activity to another without accomplishing anything except motion. When I "flit" like a butterfly, I become scattered and inconsistent.

I know where I'm going and I put my energy to good use. I focus my attention on what needs to be done now, and I do it well, rather than indulging in a variety of activities and doing nothing well. Balance and self-discipline are the key words today.

If I am not happy with what I'm doing, if I don't feel I can give my best, then perhaps I need to slow down and find out exactly where I fit, or what it is I have to offer. I have a gift to give to the world, and I put my energy to good use.

### REJUVENATION

## I WILL FIND NEW
## OPPORTUNITIES TODAY

I will view all new situations as occasions for a richer life. I will value all people I come in contact with as teachers giving lessons in survival, speaking volumes in smiles and postures, carrying whole histories in the creases of cupped hands.

I will explore my world—the sight and sound, the taste and smell and fabric of life—dazzling details missed when I mope from day to day in a safe and sterile routine.

Today I shed fears and insecurity and sharpen my senses. I sense the freshness of the world, and I undergo rejuvenation. I take off my blinders of habit and emotional constriction. I expand my vision with truth; the more open I am, the freer I become; the more honest I am, the more solid my recovery. The more aware I am, the richer my responses to life.

Today I trust and delight in my capacity for rejuvenation, and I shake off the fears and doubts that would drag me down. I will burst the confines of habit and stale routine and enter an arena alive with variety and diversity. I will feel expansion and joy in rejuvenation.

*SPIRITUAL POWER*

## TODAY I SEPARATE THE SPIRITUAL FROM THE MATERIAL

Today I will take time with myself by separating my spiritual powers from my everyday tasks and drives. I will allow my frenetic activities to come to a slow halt and allow tranquility to be felt.

This opportunity will let me usher in intense love and joy and I will appreciate that which I am often too busy to notice. I will not let my work, mail, study, house or car be in control of me today. I will feel my power, feel in control, and I'll be the one in charge of my life.

When my emotions surface, I will acknowledge them as one facet of my personality. I will examine them and freely let them happen and honestly feel them.

The goal of today is to BE—not to HAVE.

*SELF-FORGIVENESS*

## I WILL PARDON MYSELF TODAY

As I work toward a serene lifestyle, I need to be able to make amends, not only to other people, but to myself. I need to forgive myself for all the harm I have done to me.

I am important! I deserve peace within my spirit. Forgiveness assists that peace to evolve. Acceptance of my mistakes is crucial to recovery.

Today I will take time to meditate, to thoughtfully bless and forgive myself. I will start fresh and enter the rest of the day a little lighter, a little more joyful and serene.

I will remove from my vocabulary the "if onlys"—"If only I were smarter," "If only I were richer ..." I will replace those words with "I did the best I could at the time." "I made the right decision for that moment."

I want to be peaceful. I will forgive myself daily in order to open the doors to a stronger connection with my Higher Power and a serene lifestyle.

*HIGHER POWER*

### *I FEEL POWERFUL TODAY*

God provides me with all I need for today. I have different physical, spiritual, and mental needs. As I continue to gain awareness for myself in my recovery, I will continue to receive the answers I need daily.

Today I can handle all problems that arise. I need to trust my intuition and realize that God doesn't give me anything I can't handle. My Higher Power will guide me through each part of the day and will reveal to me all the meanings I need in the present. The meanings I find today will support my spirit and my strength and guide me in the right direction.

I feel powerful today.

*INNER VOICE*

## TODAY I WILL LISTEN TO MY INNER VOICE AND BE GUIDED IN THE RIGHT DIRECTION

My inner voice has all my answers loud and strong. Today I will listen to that wise part of my being that so often attempts to guide me. Sometimes this voice is firm, sometimes it is soft, sometimes it just chuckles about my interactions and my decisions.

I trust that my inner words, guided by my spiritual nature, will continually lead me on the right path. Even during times when I'm not inclined to listen, my inner voice continues to send helpful messages.

Today I will listen to my inner voice and I will be led in the right direction.

Living in an alcoholic family has often been chaotic, scary and confusing. My inner voice usually prodded me along—yet I so often chose opposite actions from what my wise part knew.

Listening to myself can guide me to serenity. Deep down inside, I know that peace exists.

I bless my inner voice today!

MOTIVATION

### TODAY I INITIATE CHANGE AND PLACE THE OUTCOME IN GOD'S HANDS

I am the main motivating force in my life. Day by day, I initiate the changes that free my emotions and enable my personality to unfold. I am the actor, not the reactor. I am comfortable with initiating changes in my life.

Growing up in an alcoholic home, I came to dread change. Change brought uncertainty, insecurity and emotional pain. I sought solace in routine and convention. Now, as an adult in recovery, I thrive on change, and I fearlessly initiate change which challenges me to grow and supports my healthy recovery.

I am at peace with the inner world of my being and with the outside world of people and circumstance. Thoughts and actions proceed from me with power and knowledge.

I am the only one who knows what's best for me. The choices I make will inspire the actions I choose. I am the one to act. My Higher Power guides my decisions and helps me carry them out.

*DISAPPOINTMENTS*

## DAY BY DAY I AM CHANGING

Today I will turn all my present disappointments into new meaning for myself. The more I venture out and take risks in business, or with male/female relationships, new hobbies, new ideas—the less fearful I become of blocks in my road to recovery. These blocks can be turned around. I can turn all disappointments into thankful learning experiences. I will also trust that my Higher Power will guide me through difficult obstacles and lead me on the right road.

In my alcoholic family, I suffered many disappointments. Now, in my recovery, I see that disappointments can teach me to be thoughtful and can spur me to persevere with my plans and projects.

I will not let obstacles set me back on my journey to recovery. Recognizing my power-filled being, I depend only upon myself to change. And I do, day by day.

SHARING

### I WILL SHARE MY GOODNESS TODAY

I will continue to share my goodness and wisdom with those who are close to me. I will not give gifts out of obligation. I will not use gifts to buy love. The love I want flows freely given from person to person, shared and generously reciprocated, no strings attached, no fine print, no "love now, pay later."

I share my goodness with others with unconditional care and appreciation. I recognize important moments and special events. I highlight them with notes of gratitude, or expressions of caring and appreciation.

Without pressure or stress, I can remain separate and still be part of the lives of my family and friends.

I will give one gift to one person today in appreciation for their place in my life.

*FUTURE*

## I WILL ENJOY TODAY AND
## LOOK FORWARD TO TOMORROW

I have complete trust in myself today. I will visualize only good in the future. All my fears will be lifted to let freedom reign within me.

Life will be fascinating in the way it will reveal new ideas to me. The better I know myself, the more available I am to new and innovative methods. There will be great positive happenings for me. I will love and be loved, be surrounded by supportive people, and I will continually choose the right path.

I will not let the alcoholism in my family block my path. I will continue to work on defining my boundaries, accepting my emotions, and taking care not to take on too many responsibilities.

I trust that the future will be rich with vigorous expression and enthusiastic experiences.

### I WILL FIND TIME
### TO DREAM TODAY

Today I will take time to dream. I will preview goals and aspirations. I will let my fantasies go wild. I know that fantasies sometimes become realities. I know that my thoughts determine the path I choose, the words I use, the people I meet. Aglow with the exciting potential of fantasy and dream, I will dream only wonderful thoughts and explore my reactions to dreams come true.

As I dream, I will dissolve the barriers and constrictions that block the free flow of my imagination. All heavy burdens, all fear of novelty and guilt for "wasting time" disappear.

This dreamtime is a time of innovation and freshness. I brush aside disparagement and criticism, and turn my thoughts into affirmations, positive statements that support and enhance my recovery. I find time to dream today, and I accept and admire my fertile imagination.

POSITIVE ATTITUDES

## I WILL HAVE A POSITIVE OUTLOOK ON LIFE TODAY

I will have a positive outlook on life today, an attitude that will allow me to experience joy and move me on a path of acceptance, love and freedom. I have the power to change the way I think. I can choose to change my attitudes, and this is what gives me freedom.

Freedom got lost in my alcoholic family. For too long I remained stuck with negative thinking and hopelessness.

Today in recovery I see that attitudes can change my thought patterns and lead me on a positive journey. My attitudes are not fixed forever; I can change them as I move through each day.

The attitudes I choose can determine my sickness or health. They can inspire hope, or they can produce despair.

Today I will change all unhealthy thinking to be healthy. I will experience the joy of the moment by my new thinking.

*LONELINESS*

## I CLAIM MY FREEDOM
## FROM LONELINESS

Today I will recognize my freedom to have fulfilling relationships with other people. I will claim my freedom from loneliness, emptiness and depression. I will greet my loneliness, face it, and set it free.

I will open my mind and my heart to the light of this day. I will choose the right people as companions, and we will share moments of the day together in love and goodness. Our words will convey a mutual respect and intimacy, and we will effortlessly communicate by voice, by touch, by smile and gesture.

I will set myself permanently free from the prison of loneliness and feelings of isolation, but I will savor the solitude that puts me in touch with my inner wisdom.

I can be alone without being lonely.

I claim my freedom from loneliness today as I appreciate the affectionate and caring people in my life.

*DECISIONS*

## I AM COMFORTABLE WITH MY DECISIONS

I will concentrate on my thinking powers today, and I will be comfortable with my decisions. I accept myself and feel worthwhile. My self-acceptance and self-worth do not depend on the opinions of others. I make my own sense of self, and I do so in full knowledge that I am a worthwhile person and that I have the ability to think and make good decisions.

I do not ask "What will so and so think?" Instead, I talk to myself, and I say: "What do I think? What do I want?" When I seek the advice of another, I do so with the knowledge that I am the one who makes the final decisions. If I try to please everyone, I end up pleasing no one at all, not even myself.

Today I will be conscious of all the little decisions I make, and I will accept all my decisions as right. I will be comfortable in my decisions, knowing that I am doing the best I can.

---

*RELAXING*

### TODAY I WILL SET ASIDE
### TEN MINUTES FOR ME

Today I will take time off from my daily routine. I will make a conscious effort to separate from work, from stress and pressure. I will give myself free time—to loaf, to notice new terrain, to have a special treat.

I never seemed to get time off from stress in my alcoholic family. It was my task to be alert and ready to cope with any emergency. There was no vacation from tension.

Now I can take time off for myself. I can take time off today to journey into new thoughts, restful interludes, new prayers of health and healing.

I will set aside ten minutes today to read, to meditate, or to simply relax. Time off helps me gain control of my own direction and sense of purpose.

*MIRACLES*

### I WILL RECOGNIZE THE MIRACLES OF TODAY

Today I will be aware of the mystic sense of wonder that God creates within my soul. I notice clouds and subtle breezes. I catch glimpses of life unfolding around me, and I am reminded again and again that each new day is indeed a new miracle.

I will treat each day as a new beginning—a fresh start—with the potential for new joy, new appreciation, new miracles. At the end of the day, when the stars sparkle in the sky, I take a brief inventory of my new learnings and experiences of the past twenty-four hours. I make those learnings part of tomorrow's miracle.

I continually grow and change by exploring that sense of wonder that was created by God to guide me on.

(202)

*SELF-TRUST*

## MY THOUGHTS ARE IMPORTANT

My thoughts will lead me on the right path. I will trust my thoughts as powerful and true today. My mind is active and alive, and it will create successful thoughts that will be guided by my Higher Power.

What I choose to think can be like dreams coming true. I will select strong, powerful ideas, and not be held down by heavy feelings. I will continually be aware of the power I have to choose my thoughts which, in turn, can lighten my feelings.

In my alcoholic family, I often did not value my thoughts enough to act upon them. I became indecisive and convinced that my ideas were worthless.

Today I will value all my thoughts and acknowledge the richness of my ideas. I will be led along the right path.

*FORGIVENESS*

### I WILL FORGIVE TODAY—
### I WILL BE FREE

Today I will forgive all those people I resent and move on to a new freedom. My resentment inhibits my energy and blocks my spirit. The rage that seethes within me affects my spirit, my emotions, and my physical well-being.

Today I concentrate on forgiveness. I do not let my rage and resentment flood out of control. I will not be blinded by emotional intensity and separated from my true strengths.

Today I will release all rage and resentment and regain my spirit by forgiving all the people I resent. I will no longer carry excess rage as excess baggage on my journey through recovery.

*PEACE*

### *TODAY I WILL FEEL AT PEACE*

Within me is an imperturbable peace. This peace is the root of my spirituality. This peace frames and reflects my mind's view of the world. This peace enables me to fearlessly trust my intuition. This peace is pure tranquility.

The spiritually-centered me is strong, power-filled, positive and alive. Love radiates from my core and shines upon all those I come in contact with. Today I will feel no turmoil, no conflict. I will not feel responsible for the thoughts and feelings of others. Centered and composed, I will be clear about my limits and I will forgive.

Perfect peace releases all stress and allows me to serenely experience all that comes my way today.

*THANKFULNESS*

## I AM THANKFUL I WAS BORN AND I'M GLAD TO BE ALIVE

Today I'm glad to be alive, I'm thankful I was born. Every day now, in recovery, I can celebrate my existence. I have a purpose. I am important. I have a place in my community. I surround myself with people who care. My Higher Power will continually guide me and make me aware of my right to be here now.

I have a mission in this life, and I take daily steps to complete this mission. My presence is essential, my presence is felt. It is difficult to be thankful when I frown upon painful events and continually feel affected by their outcome. I am responsible only for my part in life's daily tasks. I can continue to make new choices and change my path to grow in positive directions.

I am important! My ideas count, my feelings count, and I am needed! I will continually celebrate my existence.

*LAUGHTER*

## I WILL RADIATE A
## PASSION OF DELIGHT

I affirm the healing quality of laughter, and every day I catch glimpses of life, jokes, slips of the tongue, and bizarre ironies.

I can smile, I can laugh at my own pretensions. I can be frivolous and clown and walk like a duck.

Laughter works like Mr. Clean to cleanse the emotional pipes of backed up sludge. Laughter drains the body of tension and leaves it as limp as a strand of boiled spaghetti.

There are times when sadness, intense pain and anger smother the mirth and make life seem bleak and humorless.

But I am resilient, and I have the power to summon a smile and notice the comical incongruities that come each day. I can let myself chuckle at the whimsical and the ridiculous.

Today I open my mind to life's mirth and gaiety, and I let my smile truly radiate a passion of delight.

*INDIVIDUALITY*

### I WILL NOT CONTROL
### MY LOVED ONES

I will cherish my own individuality today, and I will respect the individuality of others. I will not control my loved ones, nor will I take responsibility for their actions or their words. Many times in the past, I've tried to control the alcoholic's behavior by continually making excuses for their embarrassing behavior, their blunders, their excesses and their diminished responsibility. Instead of feeling my own individuality, I felt responsible for the alcoholic's actions.

I will be strong today and concentrate on maintaining my own personhood. I will not take responsibiity for anyone else's actions or emotions.

I will be able to detach emotionally from the stresses of others. I will accept my powerlessness over others. I will accept myself, and I will accept others in their own unique individuality.

I will cherish my individuality today.

*DISAPPOINTMENT*

### *I WILL RELEASE MY DEEPEST HURTS TODAY*

Today I will find a way to release my deepest hurts so that they do not wrestle with my spirit. Many times the hurts I encounter hold me down and block my path. I need to recognize the hurt, feel it, and then discover a way to release it. The memory never fades, but the way I react to the hurt can change. Grieving the hurt will be an important part of recovery. The anger, the rage, the sadness and acceptance are steps we sometimes experience when hurt has been so deep.

When I was growing up, I often experienced hurts and disappointments. I tried to move on to new experiences and kept promising that I would never let anyone hurt me anymore. I kept letting my spirit get beaten.

Today I will begin to accept my hurt and make a conscious effort to let my spirit re-emerge with life and energy.

### *I COLLECT AND SAVOR MY SUCCESSES TODAY*

Today I take a look at my successes, and I close the book on my disappointments and failures. There is no place now for disappointment and failure in my life. I see that collecting disappointments burdens me, weighs me down, wears me out. It's like wearing lead weights on my limbs ... But when I take off the weights, when I set aside my failures to look at my successes, I feel light and full of energy.

True, as a child I was reminded often that I was a disappointment—that I had failed in many ways to meet the expectations of my alcoholic family; but now, in recovery, I'm certain that I did the best I could then.

I learn with confidence the skills that help me survive: Do I fear the water? Then I learn to swim. Do I feel helpless? Then I learn what it takes to help myself. Do I feel alone and isolated? Then I seek out new friends.

I will collect my successes and savor them.

*SPONTANEITY*

## I REMOVE MY MASKS TODAY AND I REVEAL MY GENUINE SELF

I have appeared safely incognito before others—in many safe disguises. And I now see the danger in this, the risk that I will become disguised to myself, that I will camouflage myself with thin, pleasant smiles and superficial chatter. In doing this, I counterfeit my life, disguised both to others and to myself.

I remove my masks today, for the masquerade saps me, consumes my energy, keeps me tense, guarded and apprehensive. I take a deep breath and take the plunge. I can be me, the real me, spontaneous without disguise, intimate without masks.

I accept who I am: not a fixed, rigid, cardboard entity, but a person of many moods and emotions, a person of will and talent and energy, a person of integrity and flexibility.

I can be myself today, freely, authentically and without pretense.

*DESIRES*

### TODAY I ACCEPT
### ALL MY DESIRES

Without desire there would be no growth. My ability to desire is the basis of my life. The stronger I have desires and the more clearly I understand them, the more effective my actions will become.

I will not shame myself for having desires that are inappropriate, destructive, or unacceptable. By denying negative desires, I silence the "naughty child" inside of me that needs acceptance. I can accept all my desires without acting upon them or punishing myself for daring to dream.

Today I will let my dreams and desires surface. I will not criticize or inhibit myself from letting my imagination flow. I am learning self-acceptance as I release the tight grip on my desires.

*HARMONY*

## MY INNER AND OUTER VISION ARE CLEAR—CONFUSION IS GONE

The bright dawning of this day burns away the mist of confusion. My recovery brings a lifting of the fog that has kept me uncertain of my thoughts, my feelings, and my needs. Confusion is the cloak worn by alcoholic family members.

Today, in my mind's eye, I remove this cloak and leave uncertainty behind. I can be absolutely sure about my needs and trust my feelings to help me know. As confusion lifts, I walk forward with assurance and confidence. My vision is no longer clouded, so I need not walk on false hopes or broken promises. Obstacles are not put in my way to threaten me. Rather, my vision is bright, the path before me is lit, I see the way clearly and I walk in it. With a new-found clarity, I go in peace and confidence.

*ECSTASY*

### I AM FREE TO LOVE, TO LAUGH, TO CRY OR TO PLAY

I surrender to ecstasy today. I release the tight restraints on playing, loving, laughing and crying. I feel a joy in letting go, a joy in surrender to ecstasy.

Giving up control doesn't mean that I have to be destructive or abusive. To give up control means that I surrender myself to the experience of the moment. I allow myself to be swept away by a wave, with sheer delight in my experience, knowing that I will wind up safely on shore again.

I can always choose to run from the waves with the illusion that I'll stay safe. Or I can fight the waves furiously and cling to the belief that I can win. But while I'm busy fighting and being safe, I miss out on one of life's feasts— the exquisite experience of surrender.

I will not fall into a bottomless dark pit if I give in to the moment. The dark pit is my fear, and I can face it.

Today I will surrender to joy and know that my Higher Source is with me.

CHOICE

# I WILL FEAST AT THE BANQUET OF LIFE TODAY

I have a choice to make: life can be like a lovely five-course dinner, with each course, delicious, colorful and ultimately filling; or, life can be a steady diet of fast food—temporarily satisfying my hunger, but always leaving me not quite filled up.

In order to participate in a feast, I must become willing to change and develop my taste by trying new foods. I may not like all that I taste, but I can rejoice in the experience of the banquet.

I am no longer a child, forced to eat everything whether I like it or not. I am an adult. Not only can I be discriminating by my likes, but I can even choose to leave the table. Just as grace is said over every meal, whether I like what is being served or not. I can still be thankful and appreciate the choices that are before me.

I do not over-indulge in the feast, nor do I starve myself. With the courage to experiment and my capacity to be filled with spirit, I partake of the feast of life.

*CLARITY*

### MY BELIEF AND FAITH IN
### MYSELF IS STEADFAST

How do I discover my own strength? Personal power is like an electric light switch. Unless I put my hand on the switch and turn it on, I remain in darkness. The light is there all the time, but I must do my part by switching it on to let the current flow. So it is, too, with my power.

My strength has to be used or it withers away. I must have faith in myself. I must put my faith to work, I cannot experience the full wonder and glory of life by talking about it, or by reading about it. I can't call upon someone else's strength or live on someone else's faith. I must live it myself.

Anything is possible when my beliefs are strong enough. My faith in myself will grow as I learn to demonstrate it and live by it. I do not have to wonder where my power is or where it comes from—it is there waiting to be turned on, waiting to be used.

Today I will practice my faith. I will turn on my personal power and use it in my everyday living.

*APPRECIATION*

## I SHOW MY APPRECIATION TO OTHERS AS I FULLY APPRECIATE MYSELF

Everyone I know needs to be appreciated, even as I need it from all whom I know. To be able to praise and appreciate are spiritual qualities that need to be nourished by correct thinking about myself and correct thinking about others.

Alcoholic families are expert at finding errors, blunders, and stupidity in all its members. This kind of depreciation reduces all love and joy to almost nothing. Gradually, through recovery, I am learning to think well of myself, of my loved ones and my friends.

Today I will think of the people I appreciate and say so. These people are lights along my pathway. Their faith in me increases my faith in myself. At this moment, I will think of myself in the finest terms. I appreciate those who have helped me along the way.

*BALANCE & HARMONY*

### I WILL ORCHESTRATE MY LIFE AND CREATE BALANCE AND HARMONY WITHIN

Today I stand at the podium, I raise my baton, and I conduct my own orchestra. I am organized and disciplined, and I am creative, flexible and free-flowing. I know the score. I am the singer and the song.

In the past my life was a jumble of discordant, unpleasant notes, out of tune and chaotic. There were many conductors—my parents, my teachers, and others who professed to know what was best for me. Their voices competed for my attention like an ensemble of prima donna soloists, each interested only in the sound of a single instrument—their own, their horn or violin, their voice.

But horns cannot compete with violins and expect to produce a lovely sound. The wind and strings must blend to produce a rich harmony.

I orchestrate my creativity, spirituality, physical well-being, sexuality, and emotions. With persistence and discipline, I create balance and harmony in my life.

*TURMOIL*

## *I EXPRESS MY EMOTIONS DIRECTLY*

My body is special. I will not manifest inner conflict by becoming critical of my body. If within me there exists a struggle between femininity and power or masculinity and power, I will not use my body as a psychological battleground.

It is those times when I feel inadequate, angry or depressed, that I might become too hard on myself. During these episodes, I might look at my physical image with distaste. When this happens, I become intolerant of my weight, my height, my physical presence. Perhaps self-hate and inner conflict motivate me to embark on crash diets or excessive binging.

As I read this affirmation, I become aware that my body is not the cause of the inner conflict that I may feel. With this realization, I will cease abusing or neglecting my body as a means of resolving inner turmoil. Instead, I will learn to express my emotional condition directly and articulately and avoid inflicting punishment on myself.

*CONFIDENCE*

## TODAY I CREATE A NEW GENERATION OF THOUGHTS, EMOTIONS AND BELIEFS

Today I see my life as a blackboard, and I can write whatever I choose on this blackboard of my life. Carefully I select my thoughts and erase those that do not bring me joy and peace, health and prosperity. I erase them lovingly and replace them with rewarding, productive and creative thoughts.

I am no longer that which I have erased. I am what I now write into my consciousness. I am becoming what I choose to become. I am no longer thwarted by archaic beliefs handed down to me by my family of origin.

I create a new generation of growth-producing beliefs and behaviors. I take a moment now to decide what thoughts I want to erase and what thoughts I want to create. In doing this, I begin to take control of my life.

I approach this day with renewed confidence in my ability to change.

*FAITH*

## *TODAY I WILL NURTURE MY FAITH*

Faith must be nurtured daily! We live one day at a time, moment by moment. The secret of true faith is through meditation, thought and prayer on a regular basis.

Faith is belief. Today I will renew my belief in a spiritual power, my trust in my Higher Power.

In order to nurture faith and to strengthen belief, I slowly change all my negative thoughts and reactions, change them to affirming thoughts—thoughts which enhance my recovery.

In faith, I vanquish fear. In faith, I have strength to survive times of great sadness and desolation. In faith, I find a safe path through confusion.

My recovery is a testimony to my faith in myself and in my Higher Power. My faith is the result of learning to trust, to love and to let go.

*AWARENESS*

## I AM ALIVE AND
## OPEN TO MY WORLD

Today I awaken to a world of choices. I release the old baggage of yesterday. Each situation provides new opportunities to fill my world with new ways of being. My eyes are open, my breathing is consistent, my ears are tuned to clarity. I speak my mind and "Choose Life" as I move through the day.

If I feel dull or negative about life, I am reminded that I have choices. I can change my mind and my perceptions.

I sit quietly and breathe easily. I remind myself that I am the author of my life. I release the gray and am open to the colors that will refresh me. With each even breath, with each exhalation, I let go of grayness and indecisiveness. With each inhalation, I take in new life and vital energy.

Today I feel alive and open to my fullest expression.

*RECOVERY*

# I AM MAKING ORDER
# OUT OF CHAOS

How do I put the pieces of my life back together? What do I do with those misshapen parts of myself, the parts that are old, frayed and tattered?

Recovery is the art of making order out of chaos. A person making beautiful patchwork quilts looks at many different shapes of materials and puts them together to form a work of art. A quilter will not use every piece, nor will a quilter throw odd shapes away as unfit. An artist will examine each piece to determine whether it will enhance the overall beauty of the final design.

As a child of an alcoholic, I become impatient with my own healing process. I want to get rid of all the nasty parts of myself - ..**NOW**. Any imperfect piece I want to dispose of immediately.

Let me take a lesson from the quiltmaker. I will examine all parts of myself before I make decisions to "keep" or "throw out." Who I am is all I have to work with. There is no need to rip myself apart and start over.

With love and patience, I am learning to make order out of my personal chaos. A work of art is in the making.

*RELATIONSHIPS*

## I SURROUND MYSELF WITH PEOPLE WHO RESPECT ME AND TREAT ME WELL

I no longer need to maintain abusive relationships. As I continue to grow and heal, I attract those people who love me for who I am.

I have no need to hide myself. I have no need to deny my feelings, or to disguise my thoughts and beliefs. I will no longer tolerate people who put me down, manipulate me or humiliate me. I am surrounding myself with people who are consistently loving and respectful.

Today I will pursue people with whom I can share myself in totality, with the complete confidence that they are accepting me for myself alone.

Today I have the courage to terminate relationships with people who are overly critical or not accepting of me. My world is populated with self-respecting people who radiate caring respect and consideration back to me.

SELF-TRUST

# I TRUST THE JOURNEY AND I TRUST MYSELF

Many times I have wished or prayed for things that have not been granted to me, but my desires are never in vain. Perhaps things have not changed as I have wished them to, but **always** I have changed.

There is always some change brought about by my deep yearning. Sometimes the change is in the essence of things, sometimes the change is in the essence of myself.

Oftentimes disappointments lead to new discoveries. Columbus was disappointed in his search for the Indies and discovered a new world! I, too, have had disappointments, only to discover new worlds within myself.

Being the child of an alcoholic has brought its share of suffering, but through this fate I have reached a level of awareness that might not have otherwise been possible.

Each one of us follows a path to self-discovery. None of us can see the end of the path or how the path intertwines in the larger scheme of things. Today I acknowledge that my life is more than I have the power to see or foresee.

*INNER STRENGTH*

## *I TEST MY INNER STRENGTH*

I am a student in life today, and I test my inward strength. I do not condemn myself for inadequacies, mistakes, faults or failings. My inward strength allows me to focus on my beauty, virtue and goodness, and I begin to see the beauty beyond me.

Today I will test my inner strength by seeing the positive in each person with whom I come in contact. I will also expand my vision and pay attention to nature's beauty. With the help of my Higher Power, I will draw the very best to me; I will expect the best, see the best, and focus on my own best qualities.

I have come far in my journey, and I am still a student—open to new knowledge as my understanding of myself and others expands.

*PARTNERS*

## I AM FREE TO FIND PARTNERS TO SHARE MY JOURNEY

I seek partners in family, in friends, and in lovers. I grew up feeling alone—isolated and alienated. I was not meant to live in isolation; yet, in my alcoholic family I isolated myself.

In finding a partner, I experience the joy of belonging, the quiet ecstasy of mutual nurturing.

Reaching out to touch another's hand, reaching out to listen and communicate—free me. I am sustained and comforted by my companions and soulmates on my journey through life.

*POSITIVE MEMORIES*

## I HAVE POSITIVE
## MEMORIES OF LOVED ONES

I am able to recall positive memories of loved ones today. Some of the dearest people to me have died. Today I am reminded of their attributes and their presence. Sadness fills my eyes with a feeling of loss and departure. It's so difficult at times to accept goodbyes.

When I am at an impasse, I need to remind myself how lucky I am to have been given time with friends and with my family members. God gave me the necessary exposure to my loved ones so that their impressions will live forever.

Thank you, God, for enabling me to capture some of the past—to make my life's adventures rich with experience. I am able to tap into the positive memories of loved ones today.

*SELF-RESPECT*

## I AM RESPECTFUL TO MYSELF

I will be kind to me today and center my energies on my friendship with me. I will remind myself how close I can come to destruction if I totally give away my power. With the threat of nuclear war, wars among nations, and war against myself, I need to change my attitude and bring inner peace.

In my alcoholic family, strife was always imminent. There was fighting, abrasive words, anger and blame. Today, I say "No more!" No more fighting. No more bitter arguments. No more blaming. Instead, there is acceptance, acknowledgment and peace for me.

I will talk respectfully to myself today. I will notice all of my attributes and I will be grounded in healthy directions. I lead myself to serenity, and I share my serenity with others.

CALM

### I AM CALM AND AT
### PEACE TODAY

To separate from the stresses in my life's daily schedule is my goal today. I will consciously slow down my thoughts and change my perceptions. Calmly and gracefully, I handle all that confronts me.

People, events, children, and projects will smother me and wear me down, if I let them. I need to realistically identify my limits. The only person who wears me out is me.

As I take charge and define my direction and boundaries, I will feel powerful. A renewed energy surges through me. I breathe in clean, fresh air, and I release tightness, fear and oppression. I feel calm and capable as I slow down and respect my limits.

*PURPOSE*

### IN MY JOURNEY

I have purpose on earth and I will continue to strengthen my direction. At times my direction gets confusing, and I flounder around, searching for my bearing. When I take time to remind myself that my Higher Power is guiding my journey, I feel tranquil and at peace.

Many times in my alcoholic family, my energies were blocked by my inability to separate from the emotions of others. When the alcoholic was drinking, I felt uptight, fearful and filled with anxiety. As I grew older, I began to take on the feelings of others as though those feelings were my own. I became fatigues, or consumed with busyness.

Today I will not live in extremes. I have purpose. I will celebrate the miracle of being alive, and I will feel the harmony that comes when I channel my energy into good directions.

*RENEWAL*

### *I FIND MY HIDDEN*
### *STRENGTH AND LOVE AGAIN*

Today I allow my Higher Power to take my hand and guide me to the land of rediscovery—rediscovery of my own strength and love that have been buried deep within me.

I will be able to use my strength and love to choose the path that is best for me today. Darkness will lift to let my power and direction emerge. The joy of daylight is here.

From my inner core of being, my strength and love shine forth today.

*GOOD HEALTH*

## I AM IN GOOD HEALTH

I am an expression of good health. All of life is mine to use with wisdom, joy and delight. My health is a divine gift that pervades my consciousness, my thought, my speech and my actions.

My life is orderly and peaceful. I reject all stress and tension. I am perfect strength and perfect action.

In the past I so often exhibited stressful physical symptoms. Now, as I set myself free from stress, I will set my physical self free from illness and complaints.

I respect my health and the health of my loved ones. My healthy consciousness never complains, for it is saturated with fullness and joy.

I am in good health.

*OPPORTUNITIES*

### I TURN PROBLEMS INTO
### OPPORTUNITIES

I will rejoice and give thanks today for the many opportunities I encounter. I savor the calmness and orderliness in my life. I experience each moment, each hour and each day with the assurance of serenity.

No matter what took place yesterday, no matter what takes place today or tomorrow, I am secure in my spiritual awareness that no person, place or thing can stop me from getting joy out of life. I will use each new situation to develop a deeper understanding that I don't have problems—I have opportunities.

There are no limits to my ability to think. I will open up to keener insights and sharper intuitions.

I am nurtured by love, truth and the wisdom of the spirit. I have a deep faith that I can turn my problems into opportunities for growth and fulfillment.

*MIRACLES*

# I WILL CAST ASIDE DARKNESS AND LET SUNSHINE RADIATE THROUGH ME

As today dawned, I was reminded of the miracle of life, the reality of the eternal truth— that we are all one—there can be no other premise.

Today darkness will cast aside its curtain that would hide truth from all. There is no curtain, there is no darkness. I create it all myself. When I want the sun to shine, I will use my knowledge to accomplish the light.

It isn't always easy, yet with belief in the Higher Power I will emerge from darkness and trust the new sunbeams. This glow is supported by new rules we use to usher us on in our ideas and our behavior.

I will lower my dark curtain today and peak into sunshine.

*INNER STRENGTH*

### *I WILL FEEL STRENGTH WITHIN MY OWN DWELLING*

Today I will be totally aware of my own dwelling—my home. This is my safety, my anchor, my haven. I will not feel trapped—I will feel freedom to move, to be, to create. I surround my home with acceptance and peace.

The uncertainty, anger, inconsistency and chaos in my alcoholic family made me feel trapped and anxious. My home today will surround me with gentleness, strength and freedom to be who I want to be.

I will no longer be bound in negative energy. I will change the atmosphere surrounding me by my attitude and my energy. I will give myself a physical place to be safe—my home, my anchor.

BEAUTY

## MY BEAUTY WILL SHINE FORTH TODAY

Today my beauty will shine forth and glow like the sunrise. My heart will be aglow, my soul enchanted, and my internal garden fully in bloom. I will notice my brightness shining forth and my roots taking a strong grasp in the base of my life.

I will choose only positive actions today. I will be fully aware of all my decisions and I will choose those that are best for me.

I will slow down and let my gentleness emerge. I will be at one with nature and God. I will talk tall, smile with life and notice all there is to see, all there is to smell, all there is to hear.

I will see my beauty and notice the beauty in others. A witness to today's events, I will glow and be in bloom today.

*RENEWAL*

### I WILL FULFILL MYSELF TODAY

Today I will continue my journey of transformation, and I will follow my own path to reach my destination.

Many times my journey becomes a battleground as I work to emancipate myself from the chains of co-dependency. The fight is my own internal battle with chaos and inconsistency. I struggle against the comfort I find in remaining aloof from commitments and in being over-responsible.

I push these obstacles aside. On my journey of transformation, I renew my energies by pushing negative messages aside and replacing them with messages of joy and peace.

My path follows in a positive direction. I will follow my instincts and renew my commitment to growth, transformation and self-fulfillment.

*CHALLENGES*

## I AM CHALLENGED TO OVERCOME BARRIERS

At times in the past, I thought that I would never survive. I might have been under stress at work. I may have felt tense and upset about unresolved family problems or unsatisfying relationships.

I look back and see that I have survived. I see that I can move out of tense situations by letting go of responsibility to change other people and events.

Serenity will surround me today if I don't avoid the barriers of over-responsibility thrown in my path. These barriers are my challenges, now and forever.

Today I accept these barriers as lessons in life. I challenge myself to conquer them, and I reach new heights, new realms of self-determination and inner strength.

SERENITY

## MY THOUGHTS AND MY PRESENCE WILL BE ALIVE NOW

The stillness within me has all my answers. Today I will take time to meditate, slow down and connect with the quiet wisdom of my inner self. I will use this time to contemplate my existence, my direction and my source of serenity.

Sometimes I feel overwhelmed when I ponder all the possibilities of the future—a multitude of choices all permeated with uncertainty. I get so caught up in the whirl and swirl of tomorrow that I forget to fully enjoy today.

I will take time to quiet myself so that my thoughts will not race. My thoughts slow down and I delight in the calm and serenity my quiet times bring. Guided by my calm inner wisdom, I will take my tomorrows in stride.

*SUCCESS*

# I WILL BE SUCCESSFUL TODAY

Even though my efforts at times might seem small, if they are sincere, then success is certain.

In the past, I was plagued by fears that small steps weren't enough, and that doing my best wasn't good enough. Those fears hindered my performance and invalidated my self-esteem. I need to change the messages I give myself in order to reap the harvest of rewards that are available to me.

In my alcoholic family, many times I received invalidating messages for my actions and my deeds. I need to accept that I can't change the messages that others give me. I need to change the messages I give myself in order to become freer and less self-destructive.

I surround myself with recovering positive people who will validate all of me. I tell myself today that small steps reap large rewards.

*INTIMACY*

### I AM REDEFINING INTIMACY WITH A NEW AWARENESS

Today I am sorting out my relationships with a new awareness. I have a vision of what I desire in an intimate relationship, and I am slowly making the changes necessary to get what I want.

In my alcoholic home, intimacy was confused with smothering or caretaking. In my adult life, I might have isolated myself for periods of time to avoid intimacy as I understood it.

Today I am re-defining my concept of intimacy. I am re-arranging my notions about what it means to be close to another human being. I don't have to be responsible for someone to show my love for them, nor do I have to give up my identity in order to achieve intimacy.

I have expectations of a relationship that are realistic and achievable. Allowing the one I love to be human means that I will search for happiness, not perfection. For me, intimacy is full, rich, and very possible.

*SOLITUDE*

# I WELCOME SOLITUDE AS A CHANCE FOR SELF-DISCOVERY

I am learning how to be with myself. I will no longer look for things to do just to fill my time. I can face the frightening void that sometimes lives in my soul, and I emerge triumphant.

I will not be consumed by my fear of inactivity and quiet. As I greet today, I will appreciate the calm and serenity of solitude.

I am assured that I am enveloped in the loving arms of God. I will no longer let haunting voices that threaten loneliness deprive me of the peace and comfort of being alone.

Solitude does not mean empty aloneness. I use my solitude as another channel for self-discovery.

*RESOURCES*

### I AM USING ALL MY ADULT RESOURCES AS I ENTER INTO INTIMATE RELATIONSHIPS

As the child of an alcoholic, I didn't trust intimacy. If I allowed myself to be intimate, I left myself open to rejection and abandonment. I saw models that taught me that if you cared too much, you got hurt.

Today, I see that the resources I have as an adult are quite different from the resources I had as a child. I have free choice. I can choose to enter into intimacy, and I can choose to leave if I don't like what's happening. I can choose to protect myself by going as slowly as I need to go.

Intimacy does not need to happen all at once. I will slowly give of myself and learn about myself by watching, listening, observing, and evaluating.

*TAKING RISKS*

## TODAY I WILL TAKE CHANCES

Today I'm going to take chances. I'm going to take fewer things seriously. I will dare to make mistakes and even risk being silly. I will experience special moments, one after another, instead of living many years ahead of today.

I will not be one of those people who never leave home without a thermometer, hot water bottle, a raincoat and a parachute. I am going to relax and limber up my senses. Today I will climb more mountains, swim more rivers, and eat more ice cream and less spinach.

I will experiment with taking risks that I have never taken before. After living so sensibly hour after hour, I deserve a day of great expectations. After experiencing a day like this, I may have more actual problems, but I'll have fewer imaginary ones.

*GIFTS*

## GIFTS ARE FOR THE PRESENT

I make a gift of this day to myself, and enjoy the treat, knowing that I fully deserve the richness the day has to offer.

In my alcoholic home, there was never a motivation to buy anything nice for myself. Holidays were filled with tension, celebrations were erratic, and gifts always had strings attached. My family had problems nurturing me, therefore I had problems in nurturing myself.

Today I am deserving of nice attentions. I will view myself with the eyes of a dear friend and present myself with a gift. I will experience how good it feels to have the certain knowledge that I am deserving.

*CONGRUENCE*

## MY THOUGHTS, FEELINGS AND ACTIONS ARE CONGRUENT

Today I am aware of the harmony that is developing between my feelings, thoughts, and behavior. There is a "coming together" that brings joy and wholeness to my life.

As a child, I learned to disassociate my feelings from my thoughts, and my thoughts from my behavior. No longer do I think one thing, feel another, and behave in ways that are incongruent with both. Today there is an underlying unity that allows me to glean information from all my senses before I act.

I acknowledge the value of my feelings and thoughts. I have opened the channels that provide me with the rich feedback that comes from listening, observing and feeling. I appreciate the unity that is developing within.

*ASSETS*

## I AM MY OWN BEST INVESTMENT

I am my own best investment, and just as with any good investment, I will daily monitor my mental, physical, and spiritual accounts. I will make regular deposits of time, energy and new awareness. I will regularly withdraw old patterns of feelings, beliefs and behaviors.

At times, I may become lazy, or feel hopeless and question if my recovery is worth the investment in time and energy. When my thoughts and actions fall into old patterns of anxiety and depression, I will remind myself of what life used to be like for me. With newly found awareness, I will no longer retreat into self-defeating behavior. The time and energy I spend on my healing is valuable.

I will not forget that my primary resource is myself. I will take care of this resource as a valuable, worthwhile and beautiful asset. My spiritual, mental and physical healing is a life-long investment of my time, my energy, and my love.

*FREE CHOICE*

## *I CHOOSE TO DO WHAT'S BEST FOR ME*

I have free choice, and I choose to do what's best for me. I will no longer allow my family of origin to place me in double binds. Sometimes when I come in contact with my family, the old feelings of hurt and anxiety arise. This may be compounded by the fact that no one acknowledges the alcoholism and my family members act as if everything is wonderful. All of the "no win" messages come back to remind me of how crazy I once felt.

If I choose to be with my family, I don't have to suffer through irrational messages and inconsistent behavior. I can choose to be with my family and detach myself from the old roles I used to play.

If I choose not to be with my family, I will not feel like a bad child. I refuse to feel guilty or shameful for taking care of myself.

Today I have free choice, and I choose to do what is best for me.

*GROWTH*

## I WILL GROW IN
## MANY DIRECTIONS

My growth is not limited—I will grow in many directions. I will grow deep as well as tall. When I look at a beautiful tree, I see its branches and leaves reach toward heaven. What I don't see are the strong roots that go deep into the ground to nourish and to anchor.

As I continue to grow in my recovery, I will remember that I, too, need to be anchored in reality and nourished physically, mentally, and spiritually.

I know that I can attain lofty dreams and aspirations. I can be successful; however, without a solid foundation, without roots sunk deep to nourish and anchor, my growth is limited.

Today I will grow in many directions. I will seek the depths of my being, I will attain lofty heights, and I will flourish.

*SELF-ACCEPTANCE*

## I AM A LOVABLE AND CAPABLE PERSON

In my family of origin, negative comparisons, accusations and blame were common. As I grew older, I may have taken with me a lot of self-blame.

I will no longer deal in self-contempt. I will turn down negative inner dialogue that constantly makes negative comparisons between myself and others. Shame is no longer a part of my identity.

Thoughts of my being defective or not quite good enough are being released from my consciousness at this moment. I am a lovable and capable person, and I will not reject myself.

I am not paralyzed by awareness of my limitations and mistakes; rather, I recognize myself as part of humanity that is whole and worthwhile. Through the course of my recovery, I can recognize my shame without becoming wrapped up in it.

I am learning to affirm myself from within.

*BEGINNINGS*

### *I MAKE THIS DAY A BEGINNING*

This is a time of beginning again. I will not waste my energy by looking back and longing for other days and other times. Today I have the courage to go forward in life, expecting good to unfold.

There are times when circumstances change, when relationships change, when things I have taken for granted are no longer the same. These times are times that can be extremely difficult unless I have trust in the unchanging care and guidance of my Higher Power.

Today I am ready to release every thought that binds me to the limited beliefs of yesterday. I am no longer held in bondage to the past. Today I see myself in the world, free from limitations.

*PRIORITIES*

### *TODAY I WILL MAKE CHOICES THAT ARE GOOD FOR ME*

As I enter my recovery, I am discovering that I can make responsible choices.

In the past, I may have over-indulged in eating, shopping, sex, relationships, or other activities. There have been many moments when I have been unable to stop destructive behavior. My compulsiveness resembled the alcoholic's compulsive drinking.

Today I make good decisions about what's good for me, and I hold to the decisions I make. So often in the past, my priorities have been dependent upon other people and things. When I do this, I give up my power and become controlled by outside influences.

Today I affirm my own wisdom to know what's good for me.

*RELATING*

## I RELATE TO OTHERS COMFORTABLY

I can't sit on a mountaintop and meditate to gain a high state of consciousness and at the same time forget to relate to people and things about me. I am here to grow, and my growing depends on relating to others. Isolation will not bring about my recovery. Growing into life involves an increasing awareness of my relationships on every level of experience. Every situation I face and every person I meet add new dimension to my growth. Every time a person antagonizes me or touches a "soft spot," I find out about long-forgotten emotional upsets that need my attention. I will not closet myself from people in fear of being hurt. Each step of my growth depends on how I relate to my inner and outer world.

Today I am willing and eager to relate, to interact, to understand and feel part of the WHOLE of humanity.

*EMOTIONAL RICHNESS*

**I WILL ALLOW MYSELF TO
EXPERIENCE THE RICHNESS
OF MY EMOTIONS**

Am I scared to feel? Do I still block my emotions and deny my reactions to situations? To feel sometimes takes courage. Not to feel is to cut myself off from the joy of life as well as the pain.

Imagine what life would be like if I lost my sense of touch? I could not experience heat, cold, pleasure or pain. I would be totally numb to the information and the pleasures that touch brings. I do not want to anesthetize myself from life. Instead, I will allow my emotions to enrich my life and spirit. Today, I will allow my body to tell me how I'm feeling.

My emotions are a valuable resource to me and a gift that I gratefully accept.

*SELF-EXPRESSION*

## I GIVE MYSELF PERMISSION
## TO FEEL WONDERFUL

Right now I grant myself permission to feel happier, stronger, and freer than I've ever felt before. There is no one else who can give me permission to feel good. I do not need to turn to family, friends or acquaintances for approval of my well-being. All the approval I need exists within me.

Today I am ready and willing to enter into experiences and activities that will bring about my happiness. No longer will I deprive myself of opportunities to feel good. I resolve not to let old belief patterns marshall arguments against what I am striving to do.

Today there are no critical parents in my consciousness. I have a green light to explore all the joy that I deserve to have. My permission is granted.

*WHOLENESS*

### *I SEEK WHOLENESS IN RECOVERY*

I will aim at wholeness in my recovery. Today I look at the big picture. I will examine the **pattern** of learned beliefs and behaviors that make life painful. As I strive for wholeness in my recovery, I realize that curing symptoms doesn't necessarily equate with healing.

Just as one symptom does not make a co-dependent person, so a co-dependent person does not heal by removing one symptom. This day I will take an inventory of all my symptoms, and I will begin to understand.

I am a complete human being—more than the sum of my parts, more than an aggregate of fingers, thumbs, toes, limbs and organs. As I strive for completeness, I will notice all of my symptoms with honesty and gentleness. With this loving observation, I am on the road to recovery.

*HEALTHY CHOICES*

### *I FREELY CHOOSE THAT WHICH IS BEST FOR ME*

I am totally free of any desire for things that are not for my good. The pattern I am following is healthy, satisfying, and is fulfilling to my mind, body and soul.

Many times in my alcoholic home, choices were made that were not wise. Many choices that affected me often had harmful consequences.

As an adult, I am learning new methods of caring for myself, and discovering new ways of making healthy choices.

Today my mind is free from negative thinking of any kind.

*RELATIONSHIPS*

### *I NO LONGER WISH TO MANAGE OTHERS' IMPRESSIONS*

I will cultivate self-observation, and I will see how I interact with others. Today I will set about learning how I can have satisfactory relationships—relationships that please me. In order to do that, I will observe myself in my dealings with people.

Today I will stop trying to manage the impressions that people have of me. If I have "acted" my way through life, today I will start living. People will develop whatever opinions they have of me. I will stop trying to constantly make "good" impressions. I will stop trying to impress people in order to appear more worthwhile in their eyes.

I am developing a high degree of honesty and self-observation as I strive to change.

*SOLUTIONS*

## I BEGIN THE SEARCH
## FOR SOLUTIONS

I am fully aware of the many problems that exist in being a child of an alcoholic. Problems surrounding relationships, having fun, control, trust and serenity are among the few that I have encountered. Now I am ready for solutions.

I realize there is no pat solution to my problems, but I will begin looking for answers to my many questions. To continue dwelling on my problems leaves me with little mental or spiritual healing energy. So, with full awareness of my many issues, I resolve today to begin the search for hopeful solutions.

I will begin by changing my attitudes. Today I will open my mind and my heart to new ways of being. My journey to recovery has just begun, and the best is yet to come.

*LOVE*

### *THIS DAY I WILL GIVE MYSELF THE GIFT OF LOVE*

Love is the most healing and therapeutic gift I can give myself. I do not have to reach outside myself to find love—it already exists within me. Today I embrace myself in unconditional love.

My parents, my friends, my lovers may not have given me the love I need. However, today I realize that love has never left me. It is when I don't nurture myself that I frantically search for someone to love me. This desperation leaves me as I go inside myself and discover that I AM LOVE.

Today I will open wide the door of my heart and allow the love to come flowing in. I accept this love and rejoice.

CONTROL

## I WILL DECIDE WHICH AREAS I CAN CONTROL AND WHICH AREAS I CANNOT

I must remember that life is not a constant problem to be solved. Rather, life is a mystery to be faced. I now understand why I had to keep a tight rein of control on my feelings as a child. I know why I had to believe that I could exert some control over my alcoholic family. I have accepted many unrealistic messages about what I can and cannot do.

Today I will look for opportunities to let go of control, and I will go slowly and be protective of myself. I will look for supportive and safe opportunities where I can experiment with how it feels to "let go."

Today I release my tight grip on life ... and Live!

*HEALING    RECOVERY*

## I KNOW THAT I AM RECOVERING

How do I know that I'm recovering? I know that I'm recovering because I'm standing up for myself. Nobody can put me down any more.

I know that I'm recovering because I am teaching my children to be themselves—and to be proud of it.

I know I'm recovering because I can feel.

I know I'm recovering because I'm seeing the reality in all situations. I am refusing to be hopeless about anything.

I know I'm recovering because I realize that the failure in any of my relationships was not my fault. I am not a failure because a relationship didn't work out.

I know I'm recovering because I don't have to do everything perfectly.

These signs of recovery did not appear all at once. Gradually, through time, I am noticing changes that let me know that my struggle is worth the effort.

*SURVIVAL*

### I AM A SURVIVOR

I will no longer experience life as something that "happens" to me. I have rights and I have infinite choices, but in order to attain my rights, I have to claim them. Today I will speak up and assert myself. The victim role is one I gladly cast aside, for I am tired of suffering.

By changing my label, I will change my pattern of behavior. I will no longer spend my time exchanging stories of "ain't it awful." I will no longer find myself in situations where "I have no choice." It is not my duty to take care of people by giving up my power to them.

If I have been injured, I can do something about it. Today I search for my inner strength—and I find it.

*AUTUMN SOLSTICE*

## I AM ENTITLED TO REAP
## ALL THAT I DESIRE FROM LIFE

At this fall season, I think of harvest time. I have worked strenuously throughout the year, and it is time to gather in some of the good that I have sown. Just as there has been a seed sown for every stalk of corn, so for every good effect, there was first a cause. In order to enjoy my harvest, I have had to plant healthy ideas, followed by positive actions.

At this harvest time, if I am returning home from the fields with an ''empty basket,'' perhaps I haven't given my recovery the importance it deserves. If I want to count on a consistent supply of the abundance that life has to offer, I must plant and attend to my own crops. Am I busily running about engaged in endless activity that produces little for me, or am I fully conscious of my patterns and actively involved in trying to change them?

I am deserving of an overflowing harvest. Today I will consciously plant the thoughts that will make my harvest bountiful.

*SELF-APPROVAL*

### I BELIEVE THAT I AM LIKABLE AND LOVABLE

Today I acknowledge that I have needs, and I will begin to get my needs met. I don't have to take care of people so that they will like me. Pleasing people for approval is exhausting, demeaning, and not worthy of my energy.

For so many years, I didn't admit that I had needs. It was as if I were an empty body walking around trying to grab leftovers from other people. In my mind, relationships and friendships were based solely on what I could do for others.

I declare aloud this day that I am likable and I am lovable. All I have to do is believe in myself. This is my challenge. This is my goal, and I will achieve it.

*SUCCESS*

# I ACCEPT THE GOOD FEELINGS
## THAT COME FROM
## MY SUCCESSES

I am not afraid to succeed. I will no longer snatch defeat out of the jaws of victory. If I have become comfortable with living unhappily, I hereby declare that I can succeed in a different way of living, being, and feeling.

Sometimes unpleasant conditions seem easier to cope with than the thought of change. I will not waste my energies by pursuing a life that is comfortable, but unfulfilling.

I do not have to let fear deprive me of getting what I desire. Although I might have learned much through my suffering, I know that suffering itself has no value.

Today I set a goal for myself without fear. I can succeed in my pursuit of happiness and wholeness.

*AWARENESS*

## I HAVE AWAKENED
## TO THE TRUTH

Becoming aware that something in our lives is not quite working for us is a catalyst for change. Today I realize that the only one holding me captive is myself.

The awareness that I am affected as a result of growing up in an alcoholic home is like the dawn of a new day. Now that I have awakened, I can never go back to sleep again. Now that I have given myself this gift of awareness, my past difficulties take on new significance. I now have the opportunity to learn new behaviors, new beliefs, and even new feelings.

Today I congratulate myself for this new-found knowledge. This day I will enjoy the miracle of possibilities that this awakening brings.

*ACCEPTANCE*
### *THIS DAY I ACCEPT A NEW IDEA*

Today I accept my imperfections and the imperfections of reality. A perfect universe is one which absorbs a great deal of imperfection. I feel free when I look upon reality in this way.

Today I realize that completeness contains incompleteness—that wholeness contains unwholeness. Being fully human means accepting imperfection. I can begin to accept what is and use it to become more fully human.

When I link actions with these words, I will experience no more self-hatred or self-blame over failure. This means no more recriminations or false guilt over the inevitable.

Reality is composed of endless variety. I can be easy and less demanding of myself and others when I realize nothing in life is perfect— that black or white, good or bad, rarely, if ever, exist in pure forms.

Today I let go of rigidity and panic as I marvel at the miracle of an imperfect reality.

*TIMING*

## *THE TIME IS RIGHT FOR ME TO TAKE ACTION*

Today I believe the time is right. The time for me to make decisions about my recovery has arrived. I will no longer wait to do something about my family situation, my pain, or my destructive relationships. I know that postponing help will only allow my problems to continue. If I have been waiting for the "appropriate time" to start action for my benefit, I know that the appropriate time is NOW.

If, by chance, there are children living with me, I realize that they need help too. I am no longer unsure of my needs or the needs of my children.

Today I will take care of myself. I will wait no longer for the help I need. The time has come, the moment is right.

*LOVING*

## I AM NOT AFRAID TO LOVE

I know that loving entails a desire to see and to be seen, to appreciate and to be appreciated, to explore and to be explored. These qualities are at the core of giving and receiving love.

I may not have seen healthy models of loving relationships as I grew up. Instead, I may have seen abusive relationships, people who took each other for granted, and relationships where one of the partners inevitably ended up getting hurt.

There are many couples who succeed in sustaining love over long periods of time. The excitement in their relationship is only a reflection of the excitement that exists within each of them as individuals.

I will not turn myself off and live like a machine.

I am able to love, and I am not afraid to love.

*SELF-RESPONSIBILITY*

## I AM TAKING RESPONSIBILITY
## FOR MY WELL-BEING

Recovery entails self-responsibility. No one can think for me, no one can feel for me, and no one can give meaning to my existence except me.

Self-responsibility means that I will learn to think before following unconditionally the beliefs of others. It means I will own my deepest feelings and not worry about how appropriate it is to do so. Self-responsibility means that I am a whole person whether or not I am involved in an intimate relationship. It means that I don't pretend to feel helpless or confused in order to avoid taking an independent stand.

I am an individual who is capable of experiencing a unique perspective on the world. No one else can experience my life for me. Today I take full responsibility for all that I am.

*SELF-KNOWLEDGE*

## I AM BLAZING A PATHWAY TOWARD SELF-DISCOVERY

I can learn to nourish myself and enter into intimate relationships with realistic expectations. What does it mean to nurture myself? It means that I will accept myself without reservation. It means that I will respect my own integrity and my own growth process.

To nourish myself means that I view my thoughts, feelings and desires as important. With all this in mind, nurturing means that I will create a flourishing environment for myself that promotes healthy living.

Today I have renewed respect for my internal resources. My inner strength allowed me to survive childhood and adolescence. At this moment, however, I recognize that mere survival is not enough. I want more, I deserve more, and learning how to give myself what I need is a big first step.

I will admit that I have needs. I will make decisions about how to get those needs met. I am blazing a pathway to self-discovery, and I am nurturing myself.

*REFLECTION*
# I AM MY OWN WORK OF ART

At this moment, I reflect upon the meaning of my life. I harbor within a vision of my most perfect self, a dream of what I could become. Today I will pursue this vision and work toward making my dream a reality. In this way, I will give meaning to my life.

Like an artist painting a picture, I will pause, step back from the canvas and consider what needs to be done. This will be a day of reflection. As I hope to make my life a work of art, so may these moments of contemplation help me to turn back to the canvas of life to paint a portrait of my most perfect self.

This day and every day hereafter, I will hold before my eyes the vision of what I am becoming.

*SEXUALITY*

### *I CELEBRATE MY SEXUALITY*

Sex is an act of celebration. It can be a tribute to myself and to the partner I have chosen. Today I acknowledge myself as a sexual person.

In my alcoholic home, sex might have taken on other meanings. Perhaps I learned that it was only through sex that I would be validated as a man or a woman. Perhaps I learned that sex was only a form of power that one wielded over another. I may even have been taught that "sex is dirty—so I must save it for the one I love."

I challenge all the attitudes that prohibit me from sexual enjoyment. Today I equate sex with love, benevolence and admiration.

With this new attitude, I will no longer be alienated from my own sexual responses. I will no longer separate myself from my body and pretend that what my body does has nothing to do with who I **really** am. My fantasies, my desires, and my actions are an integral and natural expression of who I am. I will experience the pleasurable integration of body and mind that sex can bring. What a wonderful means for me to experience the joy of being alive!

**(275)**

*DESIRES*

### *MY DESIRES MATTER*

My desires matter. I am not afraid to know and to express what I want. When I keep my wishes to myself, I wind up resenting other people for failing to provide for my needs.

As a child, I was taught that my desires did not matter. The fear might still exist that if I disclose to someone what I want, they might not respond—and worse, they might not care.

Today I realize that by taking the risk of expressing myself, I might not get what I ask for, but the consequences of denying my desires are more than I want to pay. I realize that no good purpose is served by being afraid to discover the truth. I will take the opportunity today to discover what I desire.

*LISTENING*

## I AM SURROUNDING MYSELF WITH PEOPLE WHO ACCEPT ME, LISTEN TO ME AND TAKE ME SERIOUSLY

What I often desire is to have someone who will listen to me and take me seriously. I don't wish to be lectured to, or told how foolish I am to feel my pain. Very often, healing is achieved through the act of expressing pain.

The greatest gift someone can give me is just to listen, merely to be available without feeling obligated to say something brilliant or to find a solution. This is the greatest gift I can offer to someone I love.

I need to silence the punitive parent that still sends me messages. I will learn to treat myself with kindness instead of with harsh, judgmental recriminations.

Today I seek out individuals who will accept me and who will listen. I do not have to live my life in silent emotional pain.

*ANGER*

## *I WILL CLEAR THE AIR WITH HONESTY*

I will clear the air with honest, open communication today. I will not deny my anger, nor will I smile while inwardly seething. I will be honest about my feelings.

When I deny or repress my anger, I remain stuck within it, imprisoned. When I'm honest enough to express my anger, I discharge this emotion and begin to move beyond it.

In the past, much of my energy has been spent trying to repress the anger I feel and making myself numb in the process. My fear of destroying relationships and alienating people has kept anger locked inside of me.

Today I acknowledge that relationships aren't destroyed by honest expressions of anger. But relationships can die as a consequence of anger that is not expressed.

Anger unexpressed kills love, kills passion, and kills relationships. This day I will clear the air with honesty.

*SELF-ACCEPTANCE*

### *I OWN ALL THAT I AM*
### *AND ALL THAT I FEEL*

Today I am willing to encounter myself. I know what I feel, and I know what motivates my actions.

In order to survive my childhood, I was taught to be oblivious to my feelings. I have learned that this alienation is disastrous for me in my adult life.

No longer do I view my thoughts or emotions as evil. My feelings are not dangerous, and I do not have to disown them nor deny they exist. Today I am reclaiming all that I disowned as a child. I am learning that people will still love me when I'm angry, and that people will still care for me when I'm helpless.

I do not have to act out or express everything that I feel, but I am free and willing to experience my emotions.

Day by day, I am creating for myself an atmosphere of respect and acceptance where I can express myself without fear.

### RELATIONSHIPS & INTIMACY

## I GROUND MY INTIMATE RELATIONSHIPS IN REALISM

My intimate relationships are based on a foundation of realism. I combine passion and insight and come up with realistic romance. I see my partner as a real person, with shortcomings as well as virtues. I will not attempt to carry on a love relationship with a fantasy. This situation is destructive to my partner and to myself. Either I will come to resent my partner for not living up to my fantasies, or I will cast myself in the role of the victim and feel outraged, betrayed and hurt.

Because I grew up in an alcoholic home, I entered adulthood with unmet needs, unmet desires, disowned hurts and longings. I do not expect a relationship to resolve or heal all my issues from the past.

I am choosing to see my partner realistically, without deception. I am aware of my deepest needs, and I enter my relationship today without the belief that all of my needs will be fulfilled. In this way, I give love and mutual respect the best of all opportunities to grow.

*AUTONOMY*

### *I RESPECT MYSELF AND
I RESPECT OTHERS*

Today I celebrate my autonomy and my freedom. I am learning not to experience myself as a child. I have grown beyond the need to prove to anyone that I am a good boy or girl. I am not waiting to be rescued or saved. I do not require anyone's permission to be who I am.

My self-esteem is secure, and I have no doubt about my worth. The source of my approval resides within me and not at the mercy of others. I possess the ability to see the normal frictions of everyday life in a realistic perspective. No longer do I translate incidents into evidence of rejection or of my not really being loved.

Along with my autonomy, I am respecting other people's needs to follow their own destinies, to be alone sometimes, to be preoccupied with issues not involved with me. I have matured to the point of being able to embrace my independence.

*HAPPINESS*

### I YIELD TO JOY

I can determine my own path to happiness. To be happy, I need to separate emotionally from my family; in so doing, I discover my inner resources. I discover my strengths.

I see that my survival does not depend on protecting my relationship with my mother or father at the expense of enjoying the rest of my life. I will not sacrifice my own happiness in order to protect my parents from feelings of inadequacy. I will not feel compelled to throw drama into my life by stirring up conflict in my relationships.

If I'm feeling content and fulfilled, I will yield to joy. I find happiness on my own terms, in my own way. I determine my own path to happiness.

*FUTURE*

### I LOOK TOWARD MY FUTURE AND EXPECT ONLY GOOD

The choices I see before me are hopeful. The future holds a variety of opportunities for growth and fulfilling relationships.

When I step back and conduct an inventory of my total life situation, the problems I have don't seem out of proportion. No situation I encounter is unbearable. If I am experiencing pain, I know that it won't last forever. I feel calm and assured when I realize that the major areas of my life are already okay and healthy.

Seeing the wonderful opportunities ahead in the future makes me feel less trapped. I am no longer a helpless child stuck in a hopeless environment. I am a capable adult, and I view the future with excitement and a sense of growing competence. Today I look toward the future and I will expect only good.

*NEEDS*

### I LIVE FROM MY CENTER

Today I am learning how to receive joyfully and without guilt. I am learning about my own needs. I am learning to take as well as to give. This day I am going to do something that's good for me.

If I can't do this easily at first, I will simply practice and see how it feels. I know that each time I learn to do something for myself, it gets easier. I will not shame myself for not enjoying myself "correctly." I must remember that I am becoming healthier, and learning to nurture myself is the best way to accomplish my goal.

Today I will accept any gifts or compliments with ease. I will not turn down any opportunity to take care of myself, as I learn how to center in on my own needs.

*HONESTY*

### I CELEBRATE MY HONESTY AND CONTINUED AWARENESS

Recovery is a process of becoming totally honest. Denial will not creep into my consciousness. I will cultivate honesty in my actions and in my words.

As a child, I sometimes tolerated extreme abuse without complaining. I learned very well how to deny my own needs and problems—how to make molehills out of mountains. As an adult, I may be carrying around the belief that if I don't admit that something is wrong, then I won't have to deal with it.

If I don't admit that a problem exists, the problem remains. Today I slowly lower the wall of denial that surrounds me. Admitting that I have problems doesn't diminish me in any way; rather, it strengthens me by preparing the way for continued awareness and growth.

*ATTENTIVENESS*

# I PAY ATTENTION TO THE
# WORDS AND ACTIONS
# OF OTHERS

I will pay attention to what people say as well as what people do. I will no longer be seduced by words without actions that are congruent.

As a child, I became used to empty threats and empty promises. My hopes rose and fell like a roller coaster propelled by wonderful words that meant nothing. But I felt then that I had to cling to any promise that invited a return of sanity and consistency in my life.

As an adult, I have sometimes become attracted to those who make wonderful promises, but who never follow through with behavior to match the words. I may have craved attention so badly that I paid attention only to the words of love and did not notice that the behavior of love was missing.

At this moment, I resolve to pay attention when what is said and what is done do not match. I will protect myself by observing the words and the behavior of those who are close to me.

*SELF-REWARD*

### BEING GOOD TO MYSELF
### IS THE BEST THERAPY

What am I doing to be good to myself? What am I doing just for fun? I will learn how to relax. I will learn how to savor time spent in rest and recuperation.

I have spent much of my time doing things for others and doing things I don't enjoy. I have spent hours doing therapy, going to therapy, working at my job, and being good to everyone else. Consequently, I became distraught, easily upset, and sometimes depressed. Like many children of alcoholics, I felt that doubling up on my workload was preferable to relaxing and having fun.

I no longer have to prove how worthwhile I am by working myself to death. Being a martyr will not win me brownie points and a sure ticket to Heaven; it will, however, make me sick, neurotic, and devoid of the joy that exists when I find time to play.

Today I give full permission to be good to myself. I will think my way into good living. I will pamper myself in small ways and observe how good it feels.

### MY LIFE IS CHANGING

As I become healthier, I desire to live joyfully, and I seek out joyful situations. Healing means that I no longer want to live in fear, indecision, or despair. If this means that I must leave a painful or destructive situation, I am free to do so.

No longer do I believe that I am supposed to suffer, nor do I believe that God is ready to punish me at any moment. These beliefs are part of the alcoholic family sickness. Getting well means acknowledging God's love and knowing that my healing is an expression of my Higher Power.

Whenever fear or despair seem to immobilize me, I will remember that these conditions are remnants of my destructive alcoholic family patterns and nothing else.

I am making daily choices to avoid beliefs or feelings that throw me back into self-defeating cycles. I am living my life based upon the firm belief that I deserve to find joy and happiness.

*PERFECTIONISM*

### I CELEBRATE MY HUMANITY

I will not focus my energies on concentrating upon every little thing that I do wrong. Do I engage in daily searches for character defects in myself and others? Engaging in perfectionism will do nothing to further my spirituality or my recovery. Today I acknowledge that only God is expected to be perfect.

Today I am abandoning any irrational guilt that keeps me trapped in destructive behavior. I am coming to recognize that spirituality which preys on my guilt can be a spiritual sickness. I do not have to participate in any obsessive behavior or thought in order to do penance for being human.

I am making steady gains in my spiritual growth as I release irrational guilt and meticulous perfectionism.

*ANGER*

# I AM FREE TO RELEASE MY ANGER OR RAGE

Today I will work on ways to get rid of my anger. I can make rational and healthy decisions about the ways I intend to express myself. Whether through counseling, keeping a journal, yelling, or confronting, I will search out a method to express myself.

One thing I will not do is internalize my anger. I will not swallow my rage by rationalizing that I was guilty or responsible for what happened to me in the past. I will keep myself free from stomach aches, backaches, headaches and other problems that result from denying my emotions.

My anger will not kill anyone. I am a powerful person—but my emotions are not powerful enough to strike someone down. For my own mental and physical health, I will change my attitude toward any unhealthy rule I have learned about blocking free expression.

I refuse to stay in a trap where I seethe in anger or wallow in depression. With a free will and a free mind, I enjoy free expression of my emotions.

*HEALING*

## AS MY HEALING PROGRESSES, I AM ATTRACTING HEALTHY RELATIONSHIPS

I am able to select relationships that are good for me. No longer am I intrigued by the "excited misery" of entering relationships with people who are practicing alcoholics, neurotics, or not very nice. If I am bored with men or women who are stable and treat me well, I will recognize that this is a self-defeating pattern.

As I experience a healing process, I am learning to feel good about myself. This means that I no longer desire to be bogged down with crazy relationships. I no longer need the turbulence that existed in my alcoholic family.

As my self-image improves, I am attracting people who treat me respectfully. Slowly, but surely, I am moving toward people who lead healthy lives—people who feel good about themselves and about me.

*SELF-PROTECTION*

### *I WILL MAKE DECISIONS IN MY OWN BEST INTEREST*

I will make decisions in my best interest today. I will no longer put up with an abusive relationship.

In my alcoholic family, I got used to living with insanity. Living with an alcoholic parent prepared me for survival. I learned to enter into destructive relationships, and then to wait and hope for the craziness to end. I learned to see a person not for who they are, but for who they might become ... **if only**

I now know that I must protect myself emotionally. I have learned that it's not safe to place my psyche in the hands of an insane person. My purpose here on earth is not to be abused emotionally or physically. It is of the utmost importance to take care of myself and to be gentle with myself.

I do not need to wait for permission to get help or to leave a relationship that is abusive. I can obtain support, but I will not wait for overwhelming approval from others for my choice. My life is my own.

SEASONS

## *I TAKE SATISFACTION*
## *IN CHANGE TODAY*

I am aware of change in myself, and I rejoice in it. My true spirit stands tall. I am strong, I am real, and I am ecstatically alive, and attuned to the world around me.

Autumn brings a ripening, a time of fruition. Autumn is mine in which to harvest all the bounty of good that surrounds me. Leaves turn color and drift to the ground. I, too, go through changes.

My soul and spirit are keenly attuned to the tug and nip of autumn, and I sense the artistry of a Higher Power in the planning and evolution of all living things. I am an integral part of nature, as unique and perfect as all else in nature that surrounds me.

I rejoice in my recovery, revel in my changes and growth that allow me to feel at home once again with nature.

CHANGES

## I AM CAPABLE OF MAKING CHANGES IN MY LIFE

I am capable of making changes in my life. I can change the situations, or I can make changes in my own beliefs, thoughts, or behavior. As I look back over my life and see the mistakes and bad choices I have made, I sometimes wonder whether I will ever be able to change this pattern of failure to one of success. I know that unlike other creatures in the world, I was given the ability to modify my program. I can't change the past, but I can alter my attitude about the present and the future.

When I experience emotional discomfort, I will learn to listen to my feelings. I will identify the source of discomfort. I will see what needs to be changed, and I will take steps to relieve that discomfort. If necessary, I will end relationships that cause me pain. I will not tolerate situations that create turmoil, anxiety and despair.

I will not remain locked in any relationship, place, or frame of mind that jeopardizes my health or my serenity. Change is necessary for growth, and I am capable of making changes in my life.

(294)

*INTIMACY*

### I SEE THE WHOLE PICTURE IN MY INTIMATE RELATIONSHIPS

In an intimate relationship, I will see both the trees and the forest. I will have a broad perspective that encompasses the infinite variety that relationships have. I will be in the present moment, and yet I will not get bogged down and lost in the details that might confront me. This means that I can love someone deeply and still be enraged with them. The validity of our relationship is not judged by moment-to-moment fluctuations in feelings.

When it comes to intimacy, it is important for me to see the whole picture. I will not participate in the alcoholic family game of "either-or"; either I love him, or I hate him; if I am angry at her, then I can't care for her; either our relationship is always exciting, or there is something terribly wrong.

Today I will not continue to freeze moments that have long vanished. When it comes to intimacy, I will experience the moment, feel it, and then let go and move on to the next moment and the next adventure.

*ALONENESS*

# I AM AT PEACE
# WITH MY ALONENESS

There are some things I must do alone. Breathing is not a group activity. Neither is thinking. I acknowledge my need for relationships, but I don't define myself totally by the relationships that I have or by the roles I play.

I must progress in my recovery by myself. I can get the love, support and assistance of those around me, but the work that I need to do can't be done by the "group." It must be done by me.

At last I am aware that my growth is up to me. Ultimately, I am facing the fact of human aloneness. This doesn't mean that I am lonely or isolated. It means that I am not resisting r denying my responsibility for my own life. Because I recognize my autonomy and responsibility, I am not engaged in dependent relationships that fill an all-encompassing void.

I see myself as a whole and complete person. I do not cling. I embrace peace with my "aloneness."

*HAPPINESS*

## I AM HAPPY AND
## CONTENT WITH MYSELF

I see that everything I need to make me happy is within myself. Today I give myself over totally to living and experiencing gladness. I know that I deserve it, and therefore I accept it.

Today I set myself free from the false belief that others have the power to make me happy or unhappy. People, places and things hold no power over me. The beliefs, feelings and behaviors of others do not intimidate me.

This moment I am free to express myself in love, joy, and enthusiasm. Through the process of my recovery, I am discovering within me all that I need in order to be happy.

I do not push or struggle for greater self-acceptance. Today I simply relax and allow my Higher Source to shine through with ease and joy.

### THE DAWN OF RECOVERY IS HERE

As I arise this morning, I open my consciousness, and I let in the dawn. For so long I wanted to live in the shadows. I preferred to lurk in darkness rather than face the light of truth. For so long I've been afraid to find out who I am. I now know that no matter what happens, I can't go back and live in darkness again.

For so Long I held in my feelings and blocked my natural self-expression. Never again will I go back to that kind of existence. My needs are real and deserve my attention. I need to be touched, to be loved, to be listened to and cared for.

And how do I get my needs met? By speaking words I've never spoken. Words like "I am," "I need," and "I feel" are now part of my vocabulary. At last, I walk into the dawn of recovery and celebrate my life.

*HOLIDAYS*

### I ANTICIPATE THE HOLIDAY SEASON WITH CLEAR AND JOYFUL EXPECTATION

This holiday season I will surround myself with people who are supportive and caring. I will not subject myself to any situation that has the potential of producing anxiety or depression. This is a joyous season and I deserve peace of mind and goodwill towards me.

I know that my attitudes and beliefs have direct bearing on my experience. I resolve to believe that I **can** and **will** have a holiday that is happy and wonderful. The kinds of negative experiences I **may** have lived through as a child during Thanksgiving, Christmas and New Year's, will not prevent me from experiencing holiday joy in my adult life.

Today I decide that whichever way I choose to celebrate this season is all right. It doesn't have to be perfect, and I will be realistic about my expectations.

As this festive season approaches, I will plan activities and be with people I enjoy. At this season I am turning my attention to my Higher Source that is showing me new ways of experiencing life.

*EXPECTATIONS*

### THE PEOPLE I LOVE
### ARE HUMAN

Today I release my unrealistic expectations of others. Today I will let go of my belief that trusting others will always bring hurt. I also turn over my belief that if someone loves me, they will never hurt me. I will no longer confuse the people I love with my alcoholic parents.

If I have been hurt by others in the past, I know it was not premeditated or intentional. I am realistic enough to know that even if someone loves me, they are, after all, human beings, and not perfect.

I do not have the emotional make-up of a child. The hurt I might experience as an adult does not have to take on the same devastating significance.

Today I resolve not to give up on intimacy because I have been hurt in the past. This day I will examine my expectations and recognize that people are, after all, only human.

*SELF-DISCLOSURE*

### TODAY I WILL COME
### OUT OF HIDING

Many times in my alcoholic family, I had to remain invisible. As a child, I was sometimes ignored—or even abused. It was too risky to show myself to the world. When I hid my true self, I found safety. I found a refuge in invisibility.

In my adult life, I've discovered that too often I am invisible to myself. I ignore my needs. I deny my emotions. I don't risk showing people who I really am.

I must remember that I can choose not to carry the pattern of invisibility with me into adulthood. I no longer have to be a victim of my biography.

Today I give myself permission to come out of hiding. I am a vital human being and I can participate fully in life without fear of punishment or other negative consequences. Today I celebrate the fulfillment of showing myself to others.

*SUPPORT NETWORK*

### I SEEK OUT OTHERS WHO CARE

Today I am not alone. I seek out others who care. There are times when I isolate myself from others by being overly critical. I will no longer express myself in this manner. I do not feel a need to rank people as being better or worse than I am. Today I put the judge in me to rest. When I do this, I begin to feel more fully that I am part of a community.

There are people in my community who would benefit from knowing me, just as I would benefit from knowing them. There are groups that I can join, where I might learn more about myself and my relationships with others.

This day I embrace the opportunity to establish a support network for myself. Today I am cultivating the attitude that it is better for me to explore than to criticize and evade people. Little by little, I am making new acquaintances and friends without being judgmental. I am not alone in this world.

*INTIMACY*

### I CAN BE INTIMATE AND
### NOT LOSE MYSELF

A healthy, intimate relationship is possible for me. When I am intimate with another, it does not mean that I will be smothered or lose myself. I will not enter a relationship as the rescuer of a drowning victim. When I function in this role, I am in danger of being "pulled under" and drowned as well. I become trapped between my desire for a close relationship and my fear of a close relationship.

Today I recognize both my desire to be intimate and my fear of intimacy. I will use these feelings to protect myself and yet give myself permission to slowly seek the closeness I yearn for.

Today I give up the notion that to be safe I must stay separate. There is no reason for me to stay isolated if I choose to be connected to another human being.

*PERCEPTIONS*

## TODAY I TRUST MY PERCEPTIONS

On this day I affirm that what I see, what I feel and what I sense are real—I can trust myself. I validate my experiences, my senses and my intuition.

As a child, I was influenced by the "no talk" rule in my family, and I came to distrust my perceptions. The constant denial that there was a problem in my home led me to believe that I was the one who was crazy. This pattern, more than any other, has caused me hurt and disappointment.

How many times have I disregarded my own warning signals? I have entered into relationships that I knew were bad for me. I have rushed into situations that I knew were dangerous. How many times must I continue to walk into the same brick wall and bruise myself?

For years I've tried to move the wall. Today I will walk in a different direction. I am learning to avoid hurt by seeing people and situations for what they are—not for what I wish them to be. I am extremely capable of perceiving what is real. I will judge what lies ahead of me and make decisions in my own best interest.

EXPERIENCES

## TODAY I HONOR THE PAST, THE PRESENT AND THE FUTURE

Today I honor the past for lessons. My experiences have brought me to a level of awareness that may otherwise not have been possible.

I can let go of resentments and realize that my parents did the best they could. As I look at the past, I feel a sense of wonder in my own healing process.

I honor the present for all the rich experiences. When I can live in the moment, I can be a full participant in life. I embrace all experiences fully, and I am available to feel a wide range of emotions.

I honor the future for dreams and visions. I am becoming the kind of person that I want to become. My ability to dream and to think magically helps me use every crisis as a vehicle to take me in the direction I want to go. When I can envision a better existence, I can embrace uncertainty with courage.

*PLEASURE*

# I HAVE THE FREEDOM TO BE INVOLVED IN MY OWN PLEASURE

When I have high self-esteem, I am concerned for my partner's happiness—I am not **responsible** for it. I want to know what my partner enjoys, without taking full responsibility for my partner's sexual happiness.

Sex is the opportunity for the sharing of love, not a means for me to prove my personal worth. When I take on the role of the "pleaser" or the "performer," I become alienated from my true thoughts and feelings. During these times, self-doubt and insecurity emerge.

How do I determine whether I'm taking too much responsibility? By expressing my desires and encouraging my partner to do the same. Just as I want the freedom to be involved in my own pleasure, I will allow my partner the same freedom. I will be guided, but not dominated, by my concern for my partner's pleasure

*HONESTY*

## I AM LEARNING BEHAVIORS
## THAT ENHANCE MY RECOVERY

When I do not feel free to express my desires directly, I sometimes try to get them satisfied indirectly, by manipulative behavior. By manipulation, I might be able to gain what I want in the short term, but in the long term I wind up creating distance rather than closeness with people.

In my alcoholic home, I learned that honest expression hardly ever produced positive results. I saw models that taught me that needs were met only through manipulation and crooked communication. In my adult life, I realize that coercing people by manipulation, by playing for sympathy or guilt, stimulates resentment.

Today I will communicate honestly. I possess the courage to be who I am and to express my thoughts, feelings, and desires. I am ready to give up manipulation as a survival strategy. I will not sabotage my recovery by reverting to dishonesty.

(307)

*SELF-RESPECT*

## I BELIEVE IN ME

I now accept that I am a channel for the infinite. I have access to a universal reservoir. Whenever I am thirsty, I honor my desire to drink, I dip my cup into the water knowing I may have as much as I can receive.

In the past, self-doubt blocked me from knowing my desires. I felt undeserving of the reservoir. My lack of faith kept me separate from the universal.

Today I accept myself as a channel. I believe in me.

*OPENNESS BEGINNINGS*

**I AM OPEN TO NEW BEGINNINGS**

Life is a cycle with an infinite number of beginnings. I enter into new situations and relationships with child-like wonder and awe. I bring my desires with me and dare to know what I would like from new encounters.

If in the past I approached beginnings with a sinking heart and fear of failure, I release the old pattern. My fear of disappointment and rejection no longer controls me. I accept my open eyes, open hands, and open heart.

I greet this day with a willingness to enter life totally. I am open to new beginnings with a joyful eagerness.

### HIGH CALIBER THOUGHTS

## I WELCOME ONLY THOSE THOUGHTS OF HIGHEST CALIBER

Today I will remember that outer disturbances cannot enter my consciousness—unless I allow them to.

As a child, I felt that I had no choice but to make my threatening environment part of my experience. This conditioning has carried over into my adulthood, and it has left me "ever ready" for attack, perhaps even in the absence of a real threat.

As of this moment, I will filter out those ideas, disturbances, and negative circumstances that impede my progress. I will lay down my weapons with the realization that I do not have to be prepared for war at all times. I simply have to acknowledge my ability to welcome only those thoughts of the highest caliber.

There is no longer any need for me to be tuned into negative influences. Today I am developing a spiritual sensitivity that attracts loving, growth-producing experiences.

CONSISTENCY

### *WHAT I SAY AND WHAT I DO*
### *ARE HARMONIOUS*

As I become healthier, I am discovering a clear sense of my own values. For years I was too busy pleasing everyone else. I had no clue as to what my thoughts, feelings, and opinions were about any situation.

Today I am willing to communicate that which I believe is important to me. Communicating my values means more than announcing my beliefs to the world. I must make sure that my actions communicate what I value. When I act unconsciously, my behavior sometimes leads to choices that contradict what I say I believe.

As a parent, as a friend, employee or lover, I will be sure that what I say and what I do are harmonious.

ASSERTIVENESS

## I AM LEARNING TO
## ASSERT MYSELF

Behavior that is enjoyable and does not inflict harm is desirable to me. Behavior that I experience as a violation—that exploits or inflicts physical injury—is wrong. I have the right to decline to participate in any act that I experience as unpleasant. Just as I must respect the taste and preferences of others, so do I expect others to respect mine.

As a child, my boundaries weren't respected. I often felt that my space, my time, and my emotions were invaded. Perhaps I learned to think that this was normal—that I was not allowed to say "No!" to anyone or anything. What I learned was how to silently tolerate inappropriate behavior.

Today I am a free adult. I am free to clearly state what I like or do not like. I am free to say what I will or will not do. I do not have to participate in any activity that I view as frightening or unpleasant. As I wholeheartedly claim this freedom, I learn to speak up and express myself.

*FAITH*

## I HAVE AN ABSOLUTE FAITH THAT MY INNER BEAUTY IS EMERGING

I remind myself today that I am a unique individual with much to offer. If I have not yet discovered my uniqueness, at least I am enjoying the quest. What keeps me from discovering my uniqueness? I find that the journey stalls only when I get in my own way.

Do I constantly compare myself with others? If I fall into this trap, I will stop and thank God for the gifts I possess. I will gently remind myself that I am not in a contest with others. Rather, I am on a journey of self-discovery.

Do I envy others for their gifts and wish I were them? This is a waste of time and energy, leading to frustration and dissatisfaction. I realize now that I have within me all I need for full expression of uniqueness.

I will not shame myself for falling into those traps. I have come a long way on my spiritual journey, and I will not be discouraged. I have changed, and I will continue to change, as I seek and discover the uniqueness that is me.

*DISCOVERY*

## I AFFECT THOSE AROUND ME IN THE MOST POSITIVE WAYS

My attention today is not on "fixing" others, but on creating a state of well-being within myself. As I discover new ways of improving the quality of my life, I can be sure that I will reflect well-being to others.

In my effort to help others, perhaps I have misplaced myself. If my life is full of contradictions, resentments, and insecurities, I might be unconsciously sabotaging the growth of those who come to me seeking help.

I must remember that as a helper, I can only be a catalyst for change. In the end, each individual must decide whether or not to embark on a different journey.

If I am critical of myself, perhaps I am quick to condemn and judge others. I must remember to disarm my own missiles of destruction that are aimed at me and at those close to me. As I develop a greater consciousness of security, support and self-appreciation, I affect those around me in the most positive ways.

*BEING CENTERED*

## I AM CENTERED, AND NOTHING CAN UPSET ME

Today I will take a moment to become balanced and to find my center. When I am centered, I am peaceful, agreeable and in harmony.

I refuse to let jealousy or pettiness enter my thinking. Throughout this day, I will experience tolerance and understanding for myself as well as for others.

Self-defeating behavior is not welcome into my consciousness today as I keep myself centered in the harmony of God's love.

I can experiment with finding out how I feel centered and at peace. In my alcoholic home, experiences of harmony and peace were foreign. Peaceful co-existence was not modeled for me.

I can choose to discover that quiet place that exists within me. I will operate from the center of my being and experience that which I long for.

*UNIQUENESS*

## I CAN BE UNIQUELY MYSELF AND HONOR THE UNIQUENESS OF OTHERS

I am discovering my uniqueness as days go by. There is no one on this earth like me. I was placed on the earth to develop that special potential that only I possess.

I look at the achievements and the specialness of others around me, and I bless them. Their wonderful qualities do not take away from my specialness. Feelings of jealousy and envy are not a part of my consciousness today.

I give dignity to myself and to those around me by ackowledging and respecting the uniqueness in others. I can learn from them, as I, too, am unique, and do not feel diminished in their presence.

*REPLENISHMENTS*

### I PAUSE TO REFLECT AND REPLENISH MY ENERGIES

Today I will take some quiet time to reflect and to replenish my energies. I will step back and disengage from the hurly-burly busy-ness of life.

I will take time to breathe slowly and deeply in tune with my natural rhythms. I will relax my facial muscles, I will relax the muscles in my arms and legs, and I will relax the muscles in my neck and shoulders.

I feel calm and at peace as I relax and breathe slowly and evenly. I leave the clamor and the stess and noise behind as I pause and let my thoughts flow peacefully.

Today I relax and take time to replenish my energies.

*FRIENDSHIPS*

# I SEEK ENDURING FRIENDSHIPS

I will surround myself today with people who care about me and treat me well. I will remind myself that friends are the people who are there for me during my pain as well as my joy. Those whom I call my friends are the ones who love me.

I don't have to bribe others to be my friends. There is no need for me to feel that I have to sleep with someone, put up with verbal abuse or pay for my friendships. If I am putting much of my energy into people who put me down, it's time to ask myself who loves me and who does not.

Today I will be selective about those whom I call my friends. I will extend my hand in friendship to those who validate me and validate themselves.

*MENTAL REHEARSAL*

## I USE MY FANTASIES AND I SOLVE MY PROBLEMS

Today I will put my fantasies to work. Instead of repeating in my mind what happened to me as a child, I picture what I would like to see happen in my adult life.

If I am about to encounter a stressful situation, I will take the time to envision the scene; I will imagine how I want to feel, how I want to behave, and how I want to be treated. Mental rehearsal will prepare me to enter stressful situations with a supply of positive feelings.

As the child of an alcoholic, I may be well-versed in fantasy. Perhaps it was through my imagination that I escaped the trauma of home. Today I can become my own nurturing parent and give myself the healthy messages I never received.

As an adult, I will put my fantasies to work. I will learn to use fantasy as a tool in my recovery to help me cope more effectively with my life.

*NEEDS*

## MY DECISIONS ARE BASED UPON MY NEEDS TODAY

Who is in the driver's seat? Am I making conscious decisions, or am I making decisions unconsciously? I see that I sometimes still have an inner child who learned unrealistic rules and who has needs that have gone unfulfilled. When faced with decisions, I must make them with the awareness of today, not based on the erratic rules of my childhood. Just as I would not allow a nine-year-old child to drive me to work, so I will not face life with my child-self in the "driver's seat."

I resolve today to make choices which are good for me. I will not feel compelled to live my life today based upon my needs of yesterday. I will decide what path to take based on my needs **today**.

*INNER STRENGTH*

### I POSSESS STRENGTH, HUMILITY AND PATIENCE

On this day, heat, warmth and light will come from deep within me. No longer will I tear the world apart to make my fire. Out of the darkness of my childhood chaos, I search for the light. I will not become a victim of cynicism and despair.

My chaotic childhood is now a memory. What happened to me then must now be woven into who I am today. I will not be discouraged by ancient memories.

I possess strength, humility and patience. I have the strength to control my compulsions, the humility to assess my own worth, the courage to rise above defeat, and the patience and trust to continue my recovery.

*SELF-ACCEPTANCE*

### I ACCEPT MY BODY

Today I will become acquainted with my body. I will pick a time and place when I can have quietness and privacy. Standing in front of the mirror, I will study myself for a few minutes. I will look at the textures, hues, shapes and designs. I am learning to see my sensuousness and my uniqueness.

I appreciate my body. I will resist participating in "ain't it awful" sessions, passing the time bemoaning how some of my body parts are too big, too small, or in the wrong place. When I strive for physical perfection, I endanger myself by entering the realm of compulsive behavior.

As I accept my body, my mind and my spirit, I move toward becoming a more balanced and whole person. No matter what kind of body I have, I am lovable and sensual.

SHARING RESPONSIBILITIES

# I CAN SHARE RESPONSIBILITIES WITH OTHERS

I will learn how to delegate responsibility. I don't have to do everything myself. By learning how to get others to help me, I will have the time to pursue activities that are important to me. I will have the time to do my own job completely and effectively.

Learning to share responsibility is important to me and to those around me. As a parent, I do my children a disservice by not delegating household chores. In work, I owe it to myself and to my organization to spread the blessings of involvement to as many people as possible.

In my alcoholic family, I trusted no one. If something had to be done, I had to do it myself. Today, this behavior is self-defeating.

I will learn to entrust others with sufficient authority to make necessary decisions. I will not play the company hero by assuming that I am the only one who can do a job well.

I take an important step toward recovery by trusting others enough to share responsibility.

(323)

COMPULSION-FREE

## I TAKE MY PLACE ON THIS EARTH WITH PRIDE AND DIGNITY

Today I will find healthy and satisfying ways to divert stressful feelings. When I indulge in compulsive behavior, it is a never-ending cycle. I will not use eating, shopping, or work as a substitute for nurturing. The resulting problems in weight gain, overspending or ill health perpetuate my low self-esteem.

Today I can be free from compulsive rituals. I rid myself of the belief that ritual behavior can protect me from deterioration. I see how compulsive behavior victimizes me and takes its toll on my loved ones.

If I am powerless over my compulsiveness, I can seek help. I don't have to do it myself. There is no secret that is so dark and repulsive that it cannot be faced. Others have done it, and I will to.

Emerging from isolation, I take my place on this earth with pride and dignity.

*PRIORITIES*

### I VALUE LOVING FRIENDS

Closeness with others is important to me. In my efforts to get ahead and succeed, I postponed getting close to other human beings. Perhaps in my role as family hero or company hero, I view relationships as a luxury I can't afford.

Today I am reminded that I am the one who sets my own priorities. Money, wealth, and success are important, but I must also acknowledge the wealth that comes from having loving friends.

I realize today that I need people I can talk to. I need people who will accept me for who I am—not for how much I earn or what position I hold.

I see that a certain amount of aloneness is inevitable on my road to success, but I will not dwell on being lonely. On my road to success, loneliness is something that I impose upon myself. I will reach out to someone today and offer my friendship.

*OBLIGATIONS*

### I PLACE MYSELF HIGH ON MY LIST OF PRIORITIES

I resolve, at this moment, to protect my priorities. I will decline requests and demands that do not contribute to the achievement of my goals. I hereby refuse to live my life according to the priorities of others.

This is the day I will weigh all my obligations. I will scrutinize my social obligations, my volunteer obligations, my chores at the office and home. I will not accept new responsibilities without weighing their cost to me in time. I do not have to prove my worth by taking on endless responsibilities.

I can learn to say "No!" in a tactful and firm way. I will cast away my fear of offending others, my anxiety about not measuring up to their expectations. The price I must pay for this kind of vigilance is far too high.

Today I will protect myself by avoiding unproductive tasks which sap my time and energy.

*HONESTY*

## I FULFILL MY
## NEEDS HONESTLY

Today I am dedicated to freely recognizing my needs and fulfilling them in healthy ways. I will not seek what I need indirectly by playing games. The longer I continue to play manipulative games, the less I enjoy doing so.

Seduction, intimidation, and helplessness are all games that were played in my alcoholic family. I am well-versed in these games, but I choose not to play along. This means that I will not run myself down, hoping for reassurance, when someone compliments me. I will not try to get attention by picking unnecessary fights.

I will enter all situations knowing that positive strokes are available to me. The beginning of obtaining what I need is realizing that I CAN get it—that it's possible and I deserve it.

*THANKFULNESS*

### I AM THANKFUL FOR TODAY

The experiences of today are here **TODAY**. There are blessings surrounding me that are meant to be enjoyed **NOW**.

I give thanks for my life, knowing that all experiences have added to my growth and understanding. I acknowledge the promise of the future, anticipating only good; however, today I center my attention on the present moment and look around my world. I see much in the way of good and much for which to give thanks.

How shall I spend my day? If I take a few quiet moments and listen to my inner voice, I will be shown how to structure my time and which activities to pursue.

And in all of my activities, I will pause now and then to reflect and give thanks. I look forward to a **NOW** filled with happiness and opportunity.

*NEW LEARNINGS*

## I ENJOY LEARNING

I can learn new things and have fun in the process. If learning to do things has always been full of pain, then it is no wonder why change has seemed frightening in the past. If I was shamed at school and at home for not doing things "right," I need to readjust my view of my own competence.

Little by little, I am becoming more certain of my intelligence and capabilities. When something interests me, I am curious and eager to learn. I keep alert to learn more about the way the world works, and to learn more about the things that influence my life.

Today I will embrace opportunities to learn new ideas. My fear of "not doing it right" is erased as of this moment. I am smart, I am capable, and I enjoy learning.

*DEFENSES*

# I WILL TAKE CHANCES TODAY

I will check in with myself through the day and find out what I'm feeling. I will be authentic—no masks, no walls to hide behind.

Defenses came in handy when I was a child. Now I see that I use defenses to keep the world away. If I am defending all of the time, I am pushing away my own life. There are so many masks that I've hidden behind, I sometimes feel as if I've locked myself away. It's hard to remember who I really am.

As I slowly let my feelings emerge, I will allow others to know who I am. No longer am I willing to pay the high price of closing myself off from my feelings. I will not hide my vulnerability from others by pretending to be someone else. I feel assured that if I show others who I really am, I will be loved and appreciated.

As I lay down my weapons, my fears and my armor, I begin to experience life. Learning to trust others and allowing others to trust me is safer than all the armor I can find.

NOVEMBER 27

*RELATIONSHIPS*

## I AM FORTHRIGHT IN
## MY RELATIONSHIPS

I am strong and capable. Any thoughts about weakness are gone today. I realize that in my home I saw many forms of control. I saw that playing "poor me" or "little child" is as powerful a weapon as forceful strength. I saw that the weak have weapons too. And I observed how emotional weapons ruined relationships.

I will not use weakness to side-step responsibility. I will not put another person in charge of my life and blame them for pushing me around. By using weakness as protection, I not only fail to make friends, I end up captive. A relationship based on protection soon withers and dies.

I want to be forthright in my relationships. I no longer have to manipulate to receive love. What I desire is to receive what others have to offer me.

Today I will trust that intimacy will flourish when what is given comes truly from the heart.

*IDENTITY*

# *I GIVE MYSELF PERMISSION TO BE WHO I AM*

I accept myself. I no longer wait for others to define me or give me permission to be who I am. I no longer need to "audition" for others, hoping that they'll see my worth. I will remember that when I pretend to be someone I'm not, I alienate others as well as myself.

Self acceptance doesn't mean that I'm narcissistic or bloated with pride. When I am really proud of who I am, I don't need to put on airs. I simply accept myself as I am and expect others to do the same.

As the child of an alcoholic, I am engaged in an honest search for myself. I embrace and cherish what I've discovered so far.

I am in the process of building a firm foundation of self-acceptance. Though self-doubt may occasionally creep into my consciousness, I know that my foundation will not crumble.

*HELPER SYNDROME*

## *I UNBURDEN MYSELF FROM THE PAST*

Today I whole-heartedly give up the burden of saving my family and saving my friends. The secret of my alcoholic home is no longer pulling me down. I am free to live my own life, and day by day I am becoming sane.

For years my life seemed like the Greek legend of Sisyphus, condemned to push a huge boulder to the top of a mountain only to have it roll down the other side. His task was endless. He toiled each day carrying the weight of the world on his shoulders.

I am tired of carrying the weight of others on my back. Today I stand straight and allow the extra baggage I've been toting to fall away.

I will not be banished by my loved ones if I live my own life. With newly found freedom, I approach this day with my shoulders relaxed, without aches and pains.

*FRIENDSHIPS*

## I CHERISH FRIENDSHIPS

I can be in a deep relationship and still maintain my other friendships. I recognize today that intimcy with another doesn't mean that I must banish my friends. Love will not be used up if it is shared.

Alcoholism isolated my family from the rest of the world. I felt cut off from my childhood friends, and yet I might be tempted to do the same as an adult.

Today I see that couples who cut off the rest of the world use each other up. Having my mate as my only friend is an awesome responsibility to place on another. I will not find fulfillment by enmeshing myself and sharing my life only with one special person.

I will not dismiss any friends in the name of love.

*SELF-ACCEPTANCE*

## I AM UNIQUE

There is no one to compare myself to and no one to compete with. When I know that I am doing my very best, I am satisfied. All notions of "better" or "worse" dissolve. When I come in contact with others, I can admire their beauty and wisdom without diminishing my own.

For years I have wished for a different body, a different personality, a different life. Now I know what a waste of time this is. I awaken to my inner beauty, and I realize my own magnificence.

Today I clearly see that there is no one to compete with—there never was. When the orchid and the rose are side by side, is one more perfect than the other?

In recovery, I am coming to see how extraordinary and incomparable I am. My interactions with others will be free from any thought of competition.

*SPECIAL MOMENTS*

## I REVEL IN THE SPECIAL MOMENTS THAT ENHANCE MY LIFE

Poignant moments make a difference in my life. When I spend hours giggling with a friend, I feel energized. When someone says something endearing to me, I feel moved. A simple compliment like "You look wonderful!" can make my day. These moments are charged with meaning and give me a special kind of energy. These are the special moments that lift my spirits when I feel down.

If I have been led to believe that life is one big disappointment after another, I will look for and remember special moments. Moments that are full and rich are abundant. I need only to pay attention and participate.

A large part of my recovery is learning to enjoy the small and beautiful gestures that make life wonderful.

*SEXUALITY*

# I ALLOW MY SEXUALITY TO EMERGE

I celebrate my emerging sexuality. I no longer have to wear loose sloppy clothes to hide my body outline. No longer do I have to appear overly prim, proper and tidy. I will not lose the support of those around me if I allow my sexuality to emerge.

I will begin today by getting some basic information. I will find out how others experience their sexuality and what they do about it. I will learn how to begin and maintain sexual relationships. I will even learn how to say "No" to sexual invitations and still feel okay.

My sexual encounters will not be futile attempts to meet the needs of a frightened, helpless child.

My sexual experiences will mature in satisfaction as I mature in recovery.

*RECREATION*

### I LEARN TO USE LEISURE AND TO ENJOY MY FREE TIME

Weekends are for my enjoyment. I will protect my time off, by not letting my work spill over into my free time. A change of pace from my rigorous daily schedule is like a breath of fresh air. I know that by allowing time for play, I contribute to my effectiveness during the week.

As a child of an alcoholic, my weekends were filled with anxiety. As an adult, I needn't keep myself busy in order to avoid my alcoholic parents. This weekend I will make an effort to remove myself completely from the problems at the office or at home. I will not become a martyr by complaining about having no time to relax. It is up to me to take time for myself.

Today I will make specific plans for recreation, and I will follow through. This week I am motivated to complete my work, so that I can enjoy my free time.

*PARENTING*

# I MODEL HEALTHY BEHAVIOR FOR MY CHILDREN

As a parent, I am participating in my child's gradual self discovery. My goal is not to "make" my child into something. My aim is to teach the skills necessary to live a full and productive life. Today I will inventory my parenting skills and become aware of my behavior.

Does my own troubled childhood lead me to suffocate and over-protect? Do I expect perfection and become critical and shaming with my own children? How often do I listen to my own voice, only to realize that it is an echo of my alcoholic parent? In my haste to flee my family, I may have brought along some uninvited "guests."

I have the opportunity to model acceptance firmness and self-esteem for my children. What a gift I have to give! My children will reflect what they have been taught, and a generation free from destructive behavior will emerge.

*ANGER*

### I AM LEARNING HOW TO RESOLVE MY EMOTIONS

I will find outlets for my rage. I will not let anger run my life.

Through the years, I have channeled my anger in many ways ... in order not to face it; I may have used competence as a weapon, exercising my power by becoming a taskmaster; perhaps I vent my anger by using chemicals or food, abusing myself and others by my erratic, destructive behavior.

I was led to believe that if I cut myself off from my rage, it would go away. Today I know that it is precisely from cutting myself off from my emotions that I lack skills in resolving them.

This is the day that I cease letting my anger run my life. I will not unjustly direct my anger toward my partner, my children, or my coworkers. When I send sparks flying every which way, it reminds me of the alcoholic's binge. Instead, I will turn to others for assistance and support.

LETTING GO

## I AM ON THE RIGHT TRACK

Life is a wonderful trip when I'm on the right track. When I let go of the heavy load of old, worn-out patterns of thoughts and behavior, I am like a train engineer who maneuvers useless boxcars onto sidetracks in order to clear the main line. There is no struggle in letting go. The boxcars of false beliefs and misapprehensions no longer have any power. They roll to a dead standstill.

I am the engineer who has a firm destination in mind. I know where I'm going, and I have confidence in the route I'm taking. The track along the way has been cleared of debris. All signals are "GO" when I know my destination. I do not allow thoughts, obstacles or limitations to sidetrack me.

Fueled by a good supply of healthy and supportive thoughts, I move surely and resolutely down the right track. The stops I make along the way will be for my pure enjoyment. As I continually express my self-acceptance, I experience love, joy, and peace in all ways.

*HERE AND NOW*
### I FULLY APPRECIATE
### THE HERE AND NOW

Time is precious and I strive to live in the here and now. At this moment, I will stop waiting for some outside person or influence to make my life better. If I continue to wait to be rescued, I might spend years waiting at the crossroad while my life passes me by.

There are many reasons to put off doing what I need to do to get on with my life. Perhaps I'm waiting for the right person to come along. Or I'm waiting for my children to grow up, or for my talents to be discovered by someone who will appreciate them and reward me lavishly.

Waiting becomes procrastination, and my excuses leave me a prisoner of the past or a passive captive of the future. Today I will think about what keeps me from improving my life.

As the child of an alcoholic, I see that living in the "now" does not mean that I can foolishly ignore my past history or fail to prepare for the future.

I know my past. I am alive in the present. And I look forward to the future.

*SELF TRUST*

# I AM DISCOVERING WHAT IS RIGHT FOR ME

I am becoming my own thinker. In order to trust myself, I must find out what is right for me. I am not here to blindly conform to what others say is fact. Some of my answers come from my ability to ask questions and not feel ashamed and embarrassed.

The greatest ideas and suggestions may not fit with my integrity, goals or purpose in life. Even ideas given by those that I dearly love might not be right for me. As an adult, I can exercise free choice. As a child of an alcoholic, I realize that this is exactly the kind of exercise that I need.

If an idea causes me to grow, then I will explore it. If a suggestion helps me to fulfill my potential, then I can accept it and make it part of my consciousness. If, in using a new idea, I find that it goes against the grain of my integrity or purpose, then I can eliminate it.

I am learning to trust myself by finding out what is right for me.

HARMONY

### I WELCOME HARMONY
### IN MY LIFE

I am learning to feel at home with good health, prosperity, and healthy relationships. There was a time when I did not feel natural when my life was running smoothly. I felt uncomfortable and nervous, as if waiting for the other shoe to drop, as if waiting for the harmony in my life to be shattered.

My thoughts and feelings were not congruent. Every time I **thought**, "I can have that"— I immediately **felt**, "I'm not deserving." I cancelled my order before it was placed.

Today I know and feel that a joyful new life awaits me. I continue to dissolve defeatist notions and I do not allow painful memories to fester in my mind.

In recovery, I welcome harmony in my life. I take pleasure in my good health and in congenial relationships. As I free myself from my old restricting beliefs, I cultivate new ideas, and I attract the highest and finest experiences. My thoughts and emotions are unified as I celebrate life today.

# I AM MY NUMBER ONE PRIORITY TODAY

I am my number one priority. I respect myself enough to set priorities that are in my best interests. I consciously release myself from the bondage of self-imposed obligations.

In my recovery, I am able to discern between fulfilling commitments out of necessity and fulfilling commitments out of duty, drudgery or guilt. I must allow enough time for myself, to fan the beautiful flame within. Quiet time, joyous time and self-expression time are necessities, not luxuries in my new design of living.

When I am my top priority, I attend to my physical, emotional and spiritual needs. Today I will schedule time to maintain my body with loving care. I will schedule time to cleanse my mind and emotions of resentments and self-destructive beliefs. In doing this, I am free to love myself, my fellow men and women, my work and my world.

---

*FULFILLMENT*

### *I FULFILL MY POTENTIAL*
### *AS THE DAY UNFOLDS*

I am alert and enthusiastic because I have great things to do this day. My sense of purpose opens wide the door that allows my energy and power to flow. My purpose in life is to reveal the nature of my higher self in whatever I do.

As the great adventure of this day unfolds, I will find that the joy of living shines through me. There is a new order in my life that allows me to fully experience love and excitement, peacefulness and harmony.

Within myself there exists all I need for this day to be one of fulfillment and success.

I have important and worthwhile things to do as the purpose of my life beautifully unfolds. My life has meaning, even in the minutest details.

And, as the sun sets on this day, I am content. I know that I am deserving of rest and peaceful solitude as I renew my spirit for the day to come.

*FREEDOM*

## I AM IN CHARGE OF
## MY UNFOLDING LIFE STORY

I hold the pen that writes my life story. I am the one who is the author of my destiny. I cannot continue to pass off responsibility for myself and still expect to live a rich and full life. When I don't take responsibility, I wind up feeling empty and dissatisfied, and my life is a continual search for reasons why.

When I am in charge of my actions, I am the one who reaps the benefits. I savor the richness and texture of life. I take immense satisfaction in living.

I affirm that I am the writer, director and star of my own play. My life will not be a Grade B movie with my name in small letters at the end of the credits. My life will be an Oscar-winning epic, a production in which I take great pride.

I have the leading role in my own life story.

*FRIENDSHIPS*
### MY FRIENDS ENRICH MY LIFE

Today, I expand my view of friendship. It is through my friends that I can see out into the world, and back into myself. I am capable of having friends who feed my spirit, feed my senses, and feed my emotions. I can be different with each friend, freely choosing the different facets of myself that I want to express.

I will not overlook the many sources of friendships that are available to me: Older people, children, people with exotic backgrounds, people with more, or less, money than I; each person has potential to enrich my life. It is possible for me to have close friends of the same sex, or friends of the opposite sex.

Today, I will remember that part of who I become is who I encounter along the way. In recovery, friends are my valuble resource.

*INTEGRITY*

## I PROUDLY INTRODUCE THE REAL "ME" TO THE WORLD

Today I will be what I want to be. I will not alienate myself from my needs and feelings by pretending I'm something I'm not. When I disconnect from my true self, I lose touch with my spirit. I become deadened and depressed and wind up throwing part of myself away.

Today I resolve to wake myself up. Living life in a trance is not what I desire. If I need to be touched, if I need attention or recognition, I will acknowledge those needs without feeling ashamed.

No longer do I need to pretend that I'm too powerful or too perfect to have needs. No longer must I "act" my way through life, hoping for emotional leftovers. At this moment, I take time to think about who I really am and what I really want.

Through the course of this day, I will proudly introduce the "real" me to those around me.

*POSITIVE ATTITUDE*

### I HAVE A POSITIVE AND VIBRANT ATTITUDE TOWARD MY HEALTH

My health can never run out. My good health is like a consistent bubbling fountain, providing me with vital energy. I appreciate my body, and in so doing, I activate the flow of positive energy.

What I think and feel produces change. My challenge today is to maximize health in my thoughts and behavior, and to know that the Divine Spirit is an active participant in my good health.

I am conscious of my good health and grateful for the freedom it creates. I extend my hands and I am aware of their ability to grasp all that I desire in life. I plant my feet firmly on the earth and acknowledge my grounding in a healthy reality. I take a deep breath and acknowledge my acceptance of positive and vibrant thoughts and my release of old, stale patterns.

As I move through this day, I have all I need to feel good. As I exercise my limits, as I breath deeply and fully, I realize that I have all I need to enjoy the days to come.

*FREEDOM*

## SOLUTIONS ARE CLOSE
## AT HAND TODAY

When I experience problems, I will remember that solutions are close at hand. Knowing this starts the flow of ideas needed to solve my problems. I know that changes do not just "happen."

Solutions involve drastic changes in thought and expectations. Solutions require action. When I am earnest about using affirmative thought, I can tackle any issue.

This day I know I am free. I can use my freedom to indulge in all kinds of negative beliefs, or I can use my freedom to discipline my mind and concentrate on finding answers to my difficulties. I choose my experiences.

Today the decision is mine.

*EXCELLENCE*

### I EXCEL AND FIND MY PLACE AT THE TOP

I am a person of integrity. I will not compromise my values and personal pride for monetary gain. Pettiness and bitterness are non-productive activities which lead to a painful lifestyle. Spending energy on revenge, or "getting back," chips away at my self-esteem.

In my recovery, my philosophy of competition is changing. The more approving I am of myself, the less I need to use hostility or put-downs in order to build myself up. I know that it is only when I am frightened or feeling inadequate that I stoop to behavior that is unbecoming to me. This means that I can be competitive and still have deep respect and caring for others.

There is no scarcity of "room at the top." Unlike my alcoholic home, there can be many winners, and I can be one of them.

With inner integrity and self-esteem, I will extend myself and strive to do my best.

### I AFFIRM MY LIFE

I am my most important critic. The only opinion vital to my well-being is the opinion I have of myself. Self-talk occurs every waking moment of my life, and the crucial briefings and conversations I have with myself are of utmost importance. The kinds of messages I give myself determine my outlook, my behavior and the course of my life.

If I was blamed and criticized as a child, my internal dialogue might be negative and self-depreciating. Today I will begin to replace my internal dialogue with healthy affirmations and improve the mental picture I have of myself. I will use positive and powerful statements about the ways I want to behave and the ways in which I want to develop.

This day marks a new beginning for me. I am through with the sarcastic negative reviewing of my daily performance. Who I see in my imagination will always rule my world. With this in mind, I will daily take the time to feed my imagination with healthy messages. The powerful image I create will be the image I project.

*RESOURCES*

### I HAVE THE RESOURCES TO MEET WHATEVER LIFE BRINGS

I have the resources to fill my inner emptiness, to light up the darkness, to turn from disappointment and despair. No one else can do that for me. No relationship, no object, no drug can fill the void that I sometimes feel.

As the child of an alcoholic, I approached adulthood feeling that "something" was missing in my life. Coming from an addicted family, I learned to look for the big "fix"—something outside myself that would take care of all pain. This belief does not work for me—particularly in intimate relationships. When I approach relationships thinking that one person will provide me with the "fix" I need to feel whole, I wind up depressed and disappointed.

I am the person in charge of bringing completeness to my life. I know how to seek advice when I need to, and I know that there are no simple "fixes" or magic solutions for complex problems.

I am freed today from yearning for someone or something to "fix" my life. I am confident in my ability to find solutions to my problems, and I have the resources to fill the emptiness in my life.

JOY

# I ACCEPT JOY INTO MY LIFE

I am ready to accept joy. I have lurked long enough in the caves of despair and hopelessness. As I dare look out, I see a different vision; blue skies, sparkling sunlight, and vibrant color! The brightness streams in, bringing fresh sights and fresh scents, and the promise of a new and fulfilling life.

My time in darkness has not been in vain. With my awareness and insight, I have illuminated the black crevices of my painful childhood. Digging into the past has expanded the depth of my feelings. I have carved out a place for myself on this earth, and I know that I have every right to be here.

Now I am ready to enter into the light. I am not afraid to laugh, to play, or to love. Soon I will be able to walk freely into the cave and out into the light at my will. Just as I have embraced my pain, so will I now embrace my joy. My range of feelings expands as I accept the loveliness of true joy.

CONGRUENCE

### I ENJOY THE SENSE OF CONGRUENCE IN MY FEELINGS AND BEHAVIOR

I have a deep desire to live congruently. When my insides don't match my outsides, I always know it. The discrepancy comes through in my behavior—small slips, irritability, nervousness, and a sense of not being genuine. When I ignore the signals my body gives me, I wind up experiencing anxiety, fear and anger.

As the child from an addicted family, I learned that the only way I could protect myself was by camouflage, by pretending to feel what I did not feel, by bravely smiling when I did not feel smiley. I learned to be a chameleon.

I no longer have to be a chameleon. I enjoy the sense of wholeness, the congruence of feelings, thoughts and behavior. Today I do not hide my real feelings behind a protective nervous grin. I smile outwardly when I feel an inner pleasure and joy. And I show my real feelings without embarrassment or fear.

*POSTURE*

# I STAND STRAIGHT TODAY AND VIEW THE WORLD HEAD-ON

I become aware of my posture today. Am I going around slump-shouldered, with my eyes fixed on the ground, as if carrying the weight of the world on my back? Or do I hold myself ram-rod erect, eyes front, chin tucked under like a Prussion soldier?

I am so much in the habit of slouching or striding like a tin soldier that I lose the natural suppleness in my posture; and as I defend myself with slumping or rigidity, I miss much of life as it passes outside my line of vision.

Today I ease the pressure from my back and shoulders. I let my body straighten, and I take my eyes off the ground and gaze at the world around me.

I move in a relaxed way, free from compulsive rigidity and hangdog slouching. My posture reflects my inner sense of competence and my feeling of being capable and at ease in the world.

*HOLIDAY SEASON*

### AT THIS SEASON, I GIVE WITH EASE AND JOY

At this time of year, I am very aware of my desire to give. I feel stimulated by the customs and activities that are so much a part of this season—the cards and carols, the sparkling lights, festivities, fellowship, warm greetings of joy and good will.

As the child of an alcoholic, I have in the past let my issues of control and perfectionism keep me from enjoying the spirit of giving at this season. I thought that my gifts must be just right, and the receiver must have the correct response to my generosity. This year, I want my giving to be different.

At this season, I will give with joy from my expanded inner knowing. I will select my gifts not to impress, but to carry my love to those who are special. Tradition has set aside the days of Hanukkah and Christmas for the demonstration of love through giving.

I will remember that material things alone are not the only gifts that express my love. Demonstrations of kindness and acknowledgment of the Divine presence in those around me are perhaps the greatest gifts of all.

*WONDER*

### TODAY I NOTICE THE WONDER OF THE WORLD AROUND ME

Where does the white go when the snow melts? Where does the wind come from? What happened to my sense of awe and wonder? In my home, I never had the luxury to wonder. It is hard to praise the creation of the world when you are involved with survival. In my "hurry up" to grow up, I missed out on some very soul-enriching experiences.

I know that the little child within me is very much alive and anxious to awaken some of my sleeping parts. The excitement and adventure for life is still available if I choose attitudes that make them so. Free from the constricting blinders of my alcoholic home, I am able to enjoy the wonderment of the world around me.

JOY

## MY TIME TO ENJOY LIFE
## IS NOW

I will relax my vigilance as I flow through the beauty of this day. Life was meant to be effortless. As the child of an alcoholic, it has taken me a tremendous amount of effort to reach this discovery.

Through much of my life, I felt like a medical resident who was "on call" 24 hours a day. I am the one who attends to every crisis, picks up all the loose ends, and doesn't sleep until everyone is comfortable. Even on my "off duty" hours, I remain on mental alert. I wonder if the doors are locked, if I said the right thing, or if perhaps I could have performed a little better. What an exhausing way to live!

Each day I promise myself that I will not be responsible for the world. Each day my resentment grows as I wait for the time when life becomes enjoyable. As I compulsively practice this lifestyle, it turns into a death style, numbing my spirit, my creativity, my zest.

Today I will allow others to take responsibility for breaking the silence at meetings, making the coffee, or making their own decision. The world will not fall apart when I cease enabling my friends, my co-workers, or my family. My time to enjoy life is NOW.

(360)

## MY FEELINGS ARE WORTH MY ATTENTION

Today I have a choice in how to deal with my feelings. My emotions are visitors that stay forever unless I talk them out or work them out. Otherwise, I will inevitably act them out. When I supress my feelings, they often show up in the form of phobias, compulsion or physical ailments.

Through the day, I will pay attention to how my body responds to feelings. If my throat is tight, perhaps I am angry. If my chest is heavy, perhaps I am sad. My body can give me much information if I don't disconnect from my physiological responses. If I have alienated myself from my emotions, today is the day I will welcome them and allow them to pass.

I realize now that my feelings are inter-related; when I can deny my sadness or pain, I can just as easily deny my joy and pleasure. When I unconsciously act out repressed emotions, I become out of touch with my own life. Today I will remember that from my feelings blossoms vulnerability, sensitivity, and healing.

*ADAPTABILITY*

## I AM RESPONSIBLE
## AND ADAPTABLE

I can recognize the limits and expectations in every situation. I know that in every circumstance there is certain behavior that is acceptable and behavior that is unacceptable. I take care of myself when I respond to limits in ways that are productive for me.

My urges to "act out" or behave shamelessly originated in my alcoholic home. It was there that I learned to confuse spontaneity with destructiveness. How many times was I embarrassed by inappropriate alcoholic behavior? It was difficult at best to find adult models who were responsible and consistent.

Today I practice the skills of healthy responsibility and adaptability. When I am in charge of my behavior, when I can adapt to existing limits, I will be more effective in achieving my goals. I will not allow my defiance or fear to propel me into embarrassing situations. Being kind to myself means learning to recognize and respond to limits.

GOOD JUDGMENT

## I USE GOOD JUDGMENT IN MANAGING MY LIFE

I am learning to use good judgment in all of my affairs. In financial matters, I will resist becoming a "five dollar millionaire" by extending my credit for short-term satisfaction. In my sexual and recreational activities, I will not overindulge myself so that I cannot carry out other necessary life activities. If I have used poor judgment in the past, I can change my pattern. Instead of shaming myself into non-productivity, I will treat myself not only with **firmness**, but also **gentleness**.

I can develop good judgment by understanding my experiences. When I can think about what happened and why it happened, I will know what steps I must take to create a different future. The mistakes I have made in the past can positively influence the decisions I make today. I only have to allow myself to learn from them.

As my self esteem increases, I am making good decisions in my own best interest.

*WONDERMENT*

### I AM AWED BY THE BEAUTY AND COMPLEXITY OF THE WORLD

I see the wonderful complexity of nature in the crystalline structure of a snowflake and in the many-faceted eye of a dragon fly. Each is one of a kind, matchless, unique. And I see that I, too, am one of a kind, matchless and unique.

I am a part of nature, part of the complex pattern of things. In times past, I have concentrated on trivial details, because the wondrous complexity of life overwhelmed me. I felt small and afraid.

I will not take life for granted, living each day as if it were one more ride on a merry-go-round. And I will not be diminished by the awesomeness of nature. Resolute and unafraid, I am making a place for myself in the world.

Today I am awed by the beauty and complexity of life.

*INVENTORY*

## I REVIEW THE PAST YEAR AND I AM PLEASED

I take an inventory of the past year, and I am pleased with my accomplishments. I see that I have made an honest effort to free myself from the tyranny of my past. I see that I have begun to treat myself with more respect. Each day I take pleasure in meeting new challenges and in finding new ways to fulfill my potential.

I have met with obstacles this past year, and I have done my best to deal with them without becoming incapacitated. I no longer have an investment in being unhealthy. I am learning to roll with the punches, and more importantly, I am learning to foresee problem areas and avoid entanglements.

I look back over the past year with a quiet satisfaction. And I look forward to the coming year with a sense of excitement and keen anticipation, knowing that I can handle whatever the New Year brings.

# INDEX